To
Amy
X
Dumo

May 2023

POEMS
1998-2023

The Pendragon Collection

2023

Poems 1998-2023

First Published through Kindle Direct Publishing

Copyright © Damian Bullen 2023

ISBN: 9798373979856

Being

Principle Memoirs & Reliques

Of

His first twenty-five years

Pass'd pleasurably in poetical composition

by

Damian Beeson Bullen

Currently dwelling on the Isle of Arran

Collated by himself

This volume is affectionately inscribed

With a triple dedication

To the General Public

To his Noble-Born Patron

& to Bards & Poets yet to be

**To the Right Honorable Michael Charles Grant,
12ᵗʰ Baron de Longueuil**

Right Honorable,

Ever since coming under your noble & erudite aegis,
my poetical mind has found an unclutter'd space in
which to create fresh compositions, & to formalize
previous effusions to my highest standards possible.
Your gift of a remarkably inspiring house on the island
of Arran, once lived in by your archaeology-loving
godfather, whose library has invigorated my
endeavors, has become the catalyst & fertile Elysian
field for the production of this humble book. I do
hope your honour will be enthus'd by such an
undertaking, proving perhaps that not *all* a poet's
hours are spent in complete idleness, & to be
reassur'd in the expectation that there will be graver
labours to come.

As the first Bard had the Baron of Titchfield, so *this*
Bard shall be in the thrall of his own member of the
Barony. I leave this book for him to survey in his own
idle hours, & perhaps remember the moments he
shar'd with the poet during certain periods of its
composition; & if he seems pleas'd, my happiness as
his humble servant will be complete

Your honour's in all duty

                              Damo

PREFACE

E l'uno il capo sopra l'altro avvala,

Perche in altrui pieta tosto si pogna,

Non pur per lo sonar delle parole

Purgatorio: Canto 13

Today marks the 25th anniversary of formally accepting my poethood. I am in a most lovely place call'd Banyalbufar, at the hotel Sa Coma, on the west coast of Majorca, under the ridiculously pretty Tramuntana range of mountains. Robert Graves is buried just up the road at Geya – the grave of Graves. My hotel has also supplied my morning with this mega edition of the Divine Comedy by Dante (OCEANO: 1992), from which I have drawn the motto for this preface, & which is serving as an excellent foil to my frothy coffees on this lofty hotel terrace overlooking the smooth blue waters of the famous Mediterranean Sea.

The contents of this book were finish'd late last night in my rooms at Esporles, before this morning I set off on a lovely topless hike up & down the ridges & paths that mark this special corner of a corner of Spain. All my personal roads have led to this moment in time & space, the Sa Coma hotel being a stunning & serendipitous find, whose further delights I am very much looking forward to investigating further. I mean, looking up the sheer stretch of rocky green from the small bay below Banyalbufar is breathtaking, a moment's suitable beauty to mark the celebration of my marriage with my Muse.

When William Hazlitt declares, *'poetry is all that is worth remembering in life,'* then surely the best poems of one's life are well worth recording, *'the deification of reality'* as Edith Sitwell put it. The creation of such a personal poetical compendium marks a moment in a poet's life when they take a deep breath & pause for a moment's reflection on the course of their career. The journey of self-realisation has taken another significant step.

Along my own journey, I have discover'd that, just as there are the Nine Modern Muses, there are also the nine avatars of Saranana, muse & Queen of Poetry. Let her be consider'd as a nine-sided crystal, slowly turning & reflecting the lights that emanate from a poet's soul.

Canzone
Sonnets
Free Verse
Odes
Ballads
Transcreation
Epyllia
Cantata
Epic

This book contains pieces conjur'd in the gaze of seven of Saranana's aspects – I have not included any transcreations, for the reason of them not being wholly mine; & epic, for being far too long. Besides, my Axis & Allies will one day be found in a tome the same size as the Divine Comedy which lies before me on the terrace of Sa Coma.

The way Saranana's awakening spirit work'd itself out within me is as follows. The *Canzone* is a short poem of only a few stanzas, the bread & butter of the art, & the form most beloved of poets who stay only as poets thro' their lives. The *Sonnet* is the king of Canzone, the cosmic camera of the world in which spontaneous moments of mentality meet the world & all its wonders. The *Cantata* is a longer version of the Canzone, Walt Whitman's *Song of Myself* is an excellent example. The *Ode* is the poet's set piece, the stitching of several Canzone together, when they turn all their powers upon the deferential appreciation of something which touches their own existence.

The *Ballad* is a lyrical history, whose tradition reaches into the very fibers of humanity. *Free Verse* is the jazz of the art, forget structure, just write... altho' it is being slowly understood that this aspect of the art has its own set of rules & forms. *Transcreation* is the conversion of another language's poem into another, not just a straight translation, which often wipes out the poetical factor X, but a new creation which held together by the mystic sinews of Saranana. *Epyllia* poems are lengthy narratives, long-measur'd often uniformly stanza'd & tell a story. Then of course there is the *Epic* avatar, given the name Calliope by the ancient Greeks, the twenty-year courtship of whom will crown the budding bard with the title of Pendragon.

As I stated at the start of this preface, POEMS 1998-2023 has been compil'd in order to mark the exact quarter-century anniversary, to the very day, in which I first truly invoked the muse in Pisa (18-04-1998). Two centuries after Wordsworth & Coleridge were putting the finishing touches to their Lyrical Ballads, I had travel'd to Italy to compose my first 'proper' poem about the Death of Shelly, living a life of roofless bohemian busking in the wine-soak'd sun. My journal of the period contains the actual moments which began it all.

Saturday April 18th, 1998

Woke up a bit rough & walk'd to the Mensa again for another delicious lunch. The rest of the day was spent kinda meandering, drinking & eating & not really making any money. Jesse play'd all day, however, & found the most amazing instrument... a fuckin' tyre inflator! It was so cool hearing him play it like a wah-wah & squeaking to the beat. Funny as fuck!

Two incidents of note happen'd during the day. The smackheads from a couple of mornings ago stole the purse of the newspaper stand lady near where we were – I got accused by the way! There was also the not so minor fact that I started to compose The Death of Shelley at last. I got two stanzas, which both roll'd so fluidly I almost had to weep. The line, *'tween the mellow, rippling fire-fields as they unfold,'* is one of the best I've ever written, etch'd in literary stone forever by the River Arno.

I'm amazed, really, to have found time during the day's crazy, lazy madness to get the energy together to write. Even so, it was a very special moment when, after traversing half the continent, I invoked. the muse in an ornate piazza neath a glorious sun.

O muse! Arise from slumber, forsake sleep,
Awake on the winds with the wings of song,
Sing blissful waves which lap as they weep
'Gainst a cluster of embraces, graceful throng,
An eternal island amongst the vasty deep
Imperial sea of the English tongue –
Come fly! bring Apollo's crown girdled in leaf,
Unshielded mine eyes, this sword I unsheath!

Whether the muse exists or not is open to discussion, but I believe that if the poet feels heady enough to acknowledge her existence & summon her to his psyche with the prayer-like incantations of an invocation, then she exists at least in the imagination, & as poetry springs from this recess of the mind, then surely she must be real.

***

Back in the Spring of 2023, the poems which fill this book, this true *'publicité singulier'* of my soul, consist of the very best pieces created in the wake of that sunny Spring day in Pisa, crossing a span of time which began in the dying analogue embers of the second Millennium AD, & concluded this morning, when I had my final editorial read thro' of this very book & sent it digitally to the publishers via the internet. Of the forty poems, of varying lengths, which I present in this book, some have been long term favorites of mine that have made every selection, others are brand new, being completed in my two years haven on the Isle of Arran. Between them, I present the poetical testament to my youth, to my art & to my engagement with the world I was born into, liv'd thro', & thoroughly enjoy'd.

Finally, here's to the next twenty-five years, in which I hope to remain physically & mentally healthy enough to create the second compendium of my life, which is already entitl'd Poems 2023-2048, beginning, perchance, on the morrow

Banyalbufar

18-04-23

CONTENTS

CANTATA

Song of the Morning
Saraswathi Song

ODES

On a tour of... Marettimo
To an Englishman with Liberty
On the Junkie Fucks of Leith

FREE VERSE

The Lost Poem
The Last Poem

CANZONE

LOVE AT FIRST SIGHT

A virgin to Eros & his sighs,
What spectral seconds suspend an eager soul,
Hearing a lute-string'd, aether seeking call,
I turn'd to see star-wreath'd & lustful eyes.

My eagle-lashed, Latvian poetess,
My pearl-eyed raven in her Persian dress,
My Spanish pea-hen spangling as she comes,
My nude Numidian banging djembe drums.

Like mountain men & archipelagos,
Or young sweethearts sniffing a first red rose,
Like money men glimpsing a glint of gold,
Or distant kin restringing at the fold;

Long time, for this fair moment, did we wait,
T'which two fair hearts attach as sure as one,
& clasping dear, as fairly dealt us fate
With rapture's gasp we match'd empyrean!

We are the music of the finches green,
We are two pussies purring by a fire,
We are the fragrance of a vernal scene,
We are two frogs full throated with desire.

We are the thistle of this bonnie land,
We are two rabbits sprinting cross the glen,
We are the seaweed strewn on sedge & sand,
We are two badgers snuggled in their den.

Like songbirds witnessing the world's first dawn,
Or parents proud who'll coo the babe's first yawn,
Like virgins witness to the breast expos'd,
Or an exploring of the always clos'd;

We are morning in the Tuscan enclaves,
We are night on the Sea of Galilee,
We are swans, gone gliding with the white waves,
For we are one in nature, you & me.

WHAT BLEEDS FOR FIVE DAYS
(& DOES NOT DIE?)

She moans about her hormones
Every second week in four,
Goes clattering the cutlery
& slamming every door.

Like when went to Sicily
& found a paradise,
But she was full of PMT
& said, *'it's not THAT nice!'*

Yet, women are man's reason,
So when swings the pendulum,
Put on your safety helmet
For the fireworks to come;

She sulks & yells, her belly swells,
Her paranoia grows,
Now fear the snarling werewolf
Where you once could sniff a rose,

'Want one?' 'No!' 'Alright,' 'Where's mine?'
'You said you didn't want one!'
'If you loved me you'd know I did – fine...'
With common sense far gone,

Like, if you feel frustrated
In a very vocal war,
Letting your lady win
Will just infuriate her more.

Cos' women synch up to the moon,
That's just the way things are,
So never say *'irrational*,
Or let her drive the car,

But when the fun is over, son,
There's one thing you must do,
Embrace your woman, kiss her lips,
& tell her, *'I love you!'*

TSU-NA-MI

Remember the host of the ghostly battalion,
Imagine them drown'd in a growling sea,
Beach-huts for driftwood, corpses for carrion,
O! sing a sad song for the TSU-NA-MI.

Remember the minute that Heaven was swelling,
When nature roars awesome in raw, rampant state,
For two-hundred-thousand
The death bell was knelling,
What Sayer or Vates foresee could their fate?

Remember the shock when the seas were retreating,
When nuclear winter on all sides was seen,
Upon the horizon the dark skies now meeting
A vast wall of water of Aegean green.

Remember the sounds on the shores of Sri Lanka,
The crunching & breaking & snapping & screams,
As ships of pig-iron are ripped from the anchor,
& pack'd teeming trains
Flung from bent, steely beams.

Remember them flock from the lush Phuket beaches,
As in rush'd a storm to destroy the fair bays,
In the wreck of Kamala street urchin beseeches
The first waves' survivors the Oceans still raise.

These scenes were a portent of deadly Katrina,
When Louisiana soon suffers deluge,
Where lives devastated by merciless water
Floats of bloated bodies flown to Baton Rouge.

Remember them fleeing those huge walls of water,
That snapp'd them & toss'd them
& made bloody piles,
The aftermath daft, she search'd for her daughter,
This sad scene repeated some three thousand miles.

Remember the grief in the streets of Sumatra,
The next Krakatoa rolls in as a gale,
The waves leave a swathe for the here & hereafter
Of death & destruction on Golgothan scale.

Remember the mood in the days after Christmas,
When so many strangers shall shun the New Year;
A new, doleful sound if the river grows restless,
Have so many tears crystalliz'd a new fear?

Remember the trail of those waves of destruction,
From Asia to Africa surg'd the wild sea,
Remember, remember, the Lord of the Ocean,
O! sing a sad song for the TSU-NA-MI.

PAISLEY

I'm cringin' every time I see
A proper Paisley tie,
I'd just popp'd hungry into Greggs
A hottish pie to buy,

& chose a steak & kidney,
Offer'd up for ninety pee,
I took the pie, she took the change
& she said, *"It's ninety-three!"*

I said, *"love, that's false advertising,"*
Stormin' out the door,
But never mess wi' Weegie Birds,
They're all fuckin' hard-core.

&, leaping from her hum-drum,
She pursued me down the street,
Looking just like an earthquake
Setting off a slab o' meat.

Then, panting, deep, beside me,
Squeez'd the pasty from mi hand,
Smugging with satisfaction
At her petty jobsworth's stand.

She turns her tail in triumph;
As back to her shop she skips,
You coulda balanced ninety-three
Bridies on 'er hips!

Then looking down on what was left,
Mi skin all bruis'd wi' mince,
I went & caught the first train out –
Ain't ever bin back since!

Chorus
Paisley, O Paisley,
I'm never going back again;
Paisley, O Paisley,
There'll never be an if,
& there'll deffo be no when!

BALLADS

THE BALLAD OF RABBIE BURNS

I never had the least thought or inclination of turning poet til I once got heartily in love, & then the rhyme & song were, in a manner the spontaneous language of my head
Robert Burns

Of poesy & her best of men
I sing, a name that maist must ken,
Its notes still sound thro' street & glen,
From fame's flaught horn;
What years are flown, twelve score & ten,
Since Burns was born.

His father'd toil'd thro' snow & sun,
Crafting a master garden,
Grafting for friendly gentlemen,
Of small estate,
Whose first born, Rab, tho' poor man's son,
Was rich in fate.

They settl'd by the gentle Doon,
With kettle-happy Granma' Broun,
Who whistl'd muckle lip-suck'd tune
While cooking neeps;
Or mutter'd tayles neath bright'ning moon
To frighten sleeps.

She spoke of mannekins, spunkies,
Of warlocks, witches, wraiths, kelpies,
Of giants, dragons, elves, brownies,
From realms faerie;
Such wyrd & wondrous trumperies
Fuels Rab's fancy.

His mind was as the green, young corn
That grows before the golden dawn,
But as Burns was a poet born,
Of no mean clout,
Like Venus in the puff of morn
His stalk stood out.

Dalrymple school would always tell
As soon as Burns could amaist spell,
He to the crambo-jingle fell,
Tho' rough & rude;
& Scotia's muse, that crooning belle,
In him renew'd.

Foregether'd with his family,
Sharing old sangs & poetry,
Or snippeting thro' history,
From Bruce to Rome;
Young Burns was bless'd wi,' luckily,
A braw Scots home!

At last, the laddie turns sixteen
At harvest coupling, when his e'en
Was fill'd with fairest country queen,
One autumn less;
She was the fairest he had seen
In dance & dress.

As lassie chimes with such sweet feel,
Rab's whining heart did wrack & wheel,
His mind riming to every reel,
With spangling pang,
From whence his soul began to deal
In sense & sang.

It fell upon a Lammas night,
When he first saw a breast fair white,
Rous'd up a lusty appetite
'Mang barley rigs,
Of how to squeeze & tease & bite
& squeal like pigs.

Soon Rabbie's loins were running free;
Leddie Peggy… dour-faced Maisie…
Fancy Jenny… easy Sophie…
Enjoy'd his charms,
While Lochiel's maid, long-lash'd Lizzie,
Adores his arms.

Yes, long-lash'd Lizzie's brash as brandy,
& in the moonlight rough & randy,
Loving a tongue-lash'd houghmagandie
With her young Burns;
Aye, both of them abed were handy,
& both took turns.

As Rab stroked her c, u, n, t,
Kiss'd slender neckline tenderly,
Twyx legs of taper white, gently,
Thrust lust inside her,
Now knowing this horn of plenty
Would spread legs wider.

Now Rabbie's handsomeness appears
Colossal in man's college years,
But working off his rent arrears,
Not stuck at school;
Debating, with his knowledge-peers,
Life's every rule.

To study mankind & its ways,
He went to many market days
Observing all life's little plays,
His teeth, eyes, hair,
Admiring lassies would amaze,
From fair to fair.

His broad shoulders made forehead's hot,
His flashing glance defences shot
&, plaided in fine fillemot,
Rab seem'd a prince;
No better man had Ayrshire got,
Nor ever since.

But, being born in poverty,
He felt his fate destin'd to be
Just hard work & obscurity
In rural climes;
But every day what poetry
Fill'd up his rhymes!

Bless Rabbie's sparks of nature's fire,
All 'twas the learning he'd desire
& tho' he drudg'd thro dub & mire
With ploughs & carts,
His muse, tho' hamely in attire,
Touch'd people's hearts.

He wove his rhymes thro' thankless work,
Or blanking out the Sunday kirk,
Or in romantic woodland walk
By Aire & Doon;
His style; 4th verse, 4th prose, 4th talk,
4th lover's croon.

Tis said all poets need a muse
To lead their souls to finer views
Of love & life, so they can lose
Dull minds in beauty;
Far prettier than psalmic pews
On solemn duty.

Now Rabbie with a lass doth clash,
His wee dog cross her wash doth dash,
On them did CUPID lightning flash
For young amour;
Pretending not to gie ane fash,
This both ignore.

They meet again that Halloween,
"Hello, I'm Rab," "Hello, I'm Jean,"
The loveliest on Mauchline green,
Leggy gazelle;
With tempting lips & roguish een
& breasted well!

At first Rab thought her wee young thing,
But then he heard an angel sing,
Watching her nimble, sma' feet spring
To beat & fiddle,
So up he join'd her in a fling,
Arms flung a-middle.

Rab woos his Jean with course romance,
Delighted by his staggish dance,
Excited by his countenance,
& dark complexion;
When clapping snapp'd the ceilidh-trance,
Lips made connection.

Meeting in secret from her pa,
Jean fell for Rabbie's gabby star,
Whose fingers shynesses unbar,
Her heart to win;
So, she lay down, long legs aspar,
& let love in.

As rubbers Rabbie rarely used,
Jean's bump her da' soon unamused,
Whose brulzie face point-blank refused
Jean for a wife;
Rab left the Armour's most confused,
& curs'd his life.

While editing his first edition,
Rab blanks out Jeanie's pa's decision,
By drinking daily to derision,
&, when frisky,
Frigs any pig, blaming his vision
On strong whiskey.

 'Hic-cup!' Rab falls on tavern floor,
Then rushes up with cavern roar,
'I, Rabbie Burns, leave Scotia's shore
To see Jamaica,
But first I'll find a local whore
& west I'll take her!'

He swiftly found his fair Mary,
A maiden from the high kintry,
Wooing her to complicity
With charming plans;
"Let's share the New World's liberty
With Scotland's clans!"

It was the second May Sunday,
When Mary said she'd *'go away'*
With Rab, upon that happy day
Their love boat sails;
Her petticoat up as they play
At heads & tails.

From Kilmarnock comes a letter,
"All is ready," says the printer,
"As publisher & editor,
You've quite a book!"
Deliver'd by its proud writer
To every nook.

With warrants out for Rab's arrest,
He heard his lass was double blest,
A boy & girl upon each breast
Call'd Rab & Jean;
So, races he, to happy chest,
Suckling serene.

His soul-woman, with their offspring,
Commenc'd his resolve's softening,
But still, determin'd west to wing
In Mary's arms,
He, with one last kiss lingering,
Left Jeanie's charms.

As Rab for Greenock dock did ride,
A message broke his manly pride,
"Young Mary has from fever died,"
Rab wails his woe;
Then sigh'd, when dewy tear ducts dried,
"Still I shall go..."

As on the road fear fill'd his heid,
For his fair Mary now was deid,
Pa Armour barring calm & plead,
There came a letter;
"The Embro gentry's all agreed
Nae Bardie's better!"

Rab, bursting from the Pentland Hills,
Would feel a thousand rousing thrills,
As clouds high Heaven's light distills
On Scotia's seats,
Where Canonsgate to Canonmills
Rose handsome streets.

Now higher Rabbie's star rising
Thro' literati glittering,
Far from a drumock's curmurring,
His voice sublime,
Distills though readers murmuring
His fresh-wrought rhyme.

They loved his love of liberty,
His heartfelt sensitivity,
His vivida vis animi,
His respect for hosts,
Scottish sentimentality,
His Haggis toasts.

As Rabbie's star was rising sun,
All of the girls would gie him one,
From Muckspreaders in Lothian
To local belles;
When maids, like Peggy Cameron,
His ego swells.

Conjoining in this celebration,
The Masons from his ain proud nation,
Gave him such a standing ovation,
The lodge roof shook,
Granting grand civic elevation
For one wee book.

Fame blossoms to the modern day,
Jock Rome drives down from Irongray
To fair Terregels, kilted, gay,
To chair the bout;
Where pipes & song & clapping bray
The haggis out!

Jock took his knife with rustic might,
"I'll cut you up wi' ready slight,
Treaching your gushing entrails bright,
Like onie ditch;
& then, O what a glorious sight
Warm-reekin' rich!"

To drunkenness the Supper swung
& Rabbie's stirring songs are sung,
Words tripping frisky from the tongue
Like birds in flight;
Harmonious, as old & young
All share the rite.

So, merry friends, let's raise a toast,
& praise the gleam of Rabbie's ghost,
Whose spirit here our hearts shall toast,
Stood hand-in-hand,
For he's the laddie loved the most
In all Scotland!

MATTY GROOVES

A holiday, a holiday,
The first one of the year,
A DJ's wife came into the club
His disco for to hear.

& when the music it came on
She cast her eyes about,
& there she saw little Matty Grooves
Dancing in the crowd.

"Come home with me, little Matty Grooves,
Come home with me tonight,
Come home with me, little Matty Grooves
& sleep with me 'til light."

"Oh, I can't come home, I won't come home
& sleep with you tonight,
By the rings on your fingers I can tell
You are the DJ's wife."

"But if I am the DJs wife
That DJ won't be home,
For he'll be up in the mixing booth
Spinning his silver chrome!"

So off they went into the night,
& hail'd a taxi down
Then partied on at the DJ's pad
At the other side of town.

& the waitress who'd been watchin' on
& heard just what was said,
Swore down that the DJ he would know
At the spinning of his set.

"O Matty Grooves, O Matty Grooves,
O Matty where have ye gone?"
"I've gone to play with the DJs wife
'Til the rise of the morning sun."

Little Matty Grooves he made good love,
Then took a little sleep,
& when he woke a coked-up bloke
Stood fuming at his feet.

Saying, *"How do you like my feather bed?*
& how do you like my sheets?
& how do you like my lady wife
Who lies in your arms asleep?"

"Oh, well I like your feather bed,
& brother I love your sheets,
But better I like your lady wife
Who lies in my arms asleep."

"Get up, get dress'd!" the DJ cried,
"Get up as quick as you can,
It'll never be said in Edinburgh
I slew a naked man."

"Oh, I can't get up, I won't get up,
I can't get up for my life,
Its true that ya got two 'Wallace' swords
& I ain't got a pocket knife."

"Well, it's true that I got two 'Wallace' Swords
& they cost me deep in the purse,
But you will have the better of them
& I will have the worse."

"& you will strike the very first blow
& strike it like a man,
Then I will strike the very next blow
& kill you if I can"

"O Matty Grooves, O Matty Grooves,
O Matty what have ye done?"
"I was making love to the DJs wife
'Til the rise of the morning sun."

So Matty struck the very first blow
& he hurt that DJ sore,
The DJ struck the very next blow
& Matty struck no more.

The smurkin' DJ jerks his wife
& perch'd her upon his knee,
Saying, *"who do you like the best of us,*
That Matty Grooves or me?"

& so up-spoke his own dear wife,
Never heard to speak so free,
"I'd rather a kiss from dead Matty's lips
Than you or your finery."

The DJ he did flummox up
& loudly he did bawl,
Then struck his wife with a Wallace knife
& stuck her into the wall.

"A grave, a grave," the DJ cried,
"To put these lovers in!"
& struts up to his technik turntables,
His best set yet to spin.

Where picking up his mobile phone
He's dialling 9-9-9,
& said, *"my lady wife is dead*
& I'll confess to the crime!"

While raving top-blast to his tunes,
His faves of Mr Scruff's,
The Fuzz burst in his blood-red gaff
& dragg'd him off in cuffs.

"O Matty Grooves, O Matty Grooves,
O Matty where have ye gone?
Since you went off with a DJs wife,
You'll never more see the sun!"

OVER THE TOP: Loos, 1915

The greatest battle of the Scots
Lurches towards its breaking,
Thoughts clawing stomach pits in knots,
'How long's the twilight taking?'

Puffing under the parapet's
Immovable rampart,
One hundred thousand cigarettes
Await the gig to start.

As to them *Zero Hour* doth sweep
On hooves of adamant,
Captain's boom out, with vocals deep,
To every regiment;

'All ranks will prove to Scotland, we
Were able to uphold
Traditions of the north contree,
Most glorious of auld!

For Highlanders have ever been
The finest of all fighters,
Whether fae chieftain, prince, or queen,
No force could e'er out-might us."

The barrage halts, the silence sets,
The seconds overloaded,
'Company – fix bayonets,'
Throughout the front line order'd.

As sharpen'd spikes were firmly fix'd,
A sudden infestation
Of polarised emotions mix'd -
Hysteria, exultation.

'Is everybody ready?' 'Sir!'
As back hairs, neck hairs bristle,
At last the drastic brainwaves' blur,
Attacks the straining whistle.

Up, up, the ladders & over the top,
Up over the top they went,
The finest chop of the Highland crop
To ever represent.

Up over the top with the best of luck,
Up over the top they sped,
The first man up by a bullet struck
& dropp'd down dead.

Up over the top, & onto the plain,
Then over the grain them borne,
Where barb'd wire bush in a bramble bane
Spread like the low lean thorn.

When sighting Hohenzollorn mound
Ahead, men caught their breath,
Amang that slag-heap battleground,
They'll jest at the dawn with death.

How hard had train'd true-hearted men
For this elusive moment;
On, steady, in platoons of ten,
The Black Watch went.

Across the way the Germans say,
'The moles have left their holes,'
Whom with a sweeping bullet spray
This steady progress stalls.

A tumbling here, a stumbling there,
As crumbling the advance
Once solid mass now spaced with air,
Unsewn by happenstance.

A rat-a-tat, a rat-a-tat,
& rat-a-tat Death roams,
Lead scattering this way & that
In gory honeycombs.

With rat-a-tat along the line
Men batter'd broke & bleeding,
Grass splattering with claret wine
By men for mothers pleading,

Those parents who had paid the tolls
Of lifetimes, for their boys,
Only to turn to lifeless dolls,
Like royalty's toys.

'O tis a terrifying thing
To walk towards one's death,
This step I take, is there a sting,
Is this my final breath?'

Thought George, then drops, a boy's clean cheeks
Beside, whose face was flapping,
'I'll be alright,' soft Doric creaks,
As if awoke from napping.

For glorious assault was theirs,
'I'm wounded but not slain…
I'll lie awhile,' the lad declares,
'Then rise & fight again.'

From out beyond the Loss-Lens lines,
Enemy artillery
Shoots shrapnel spines of porcupines,
To this savage pillory

Of jagged iron insanities,
Exploding flagellant,
To level off the vanities
With sinister intent.

Sharp-pointed lead-barbs struck the Watch
In legs, in arms, in head,
In chest, in throat, in knees, in crotch
In foot, in jaws… as bled

Deep seeping into Flanders soil
The bloodlines of the Scottish,
Gone swaggering into the boil
Of bullets swish-swish-swish.

As murder's prattling rattles peak
At life & limbs exacting,
As eyeballs rest upon the cheek,
Lungs in & out contracting –

Most horrendous exhibitions
Of complex anatomy,
Crudely sculptur'd by munitions
Of this vicious enemy.

Despite the firestorm's withering,
No thought was sought fae stopping,
Leg-wounded lads, unswithering,
Still forwards go, hop-hopping,

When following their leaders on
Thro' terror's vaults unseal'd,
Exhorting leaders, one-by-one,
Caught death upon that field.

For 'mercy' screams Lieutenant Hailes,
Clutching his stomach's squirting,
For morphia he begs & wails,
Awfully disconcerting.

Tho' Major Henderson's concuss,
& noble bloodflow slowing,
Strength found enough to raise his puss,
'Pure barry lads, keep going!'

As Wullie McIntyre did stride
Into that cry & hue,
Men fallen off on either side
& now he takes one too.

He hit the ground, he tasted dust,
He knew his life was ending,
His plans of youth & age all crush'd,
The cloak of death descending.

He hit the ground, he smelt the earth,
He felt each fiber dying,
Long flashback to his babybirth,
Like then he started crying

For Arran's large & lofty crags
Rose up so splendid grand
Inside his mind, while antler'd stags
Did silhouetted stand.

Then, conjur'd he Kildonan strand;
There's Ailsa Craig, there's Pladda,
As lighthouse lit the lantern sand
Each second soul slain sadder,

Until he saw a silver light
Moonshining, astral zones
Like temples spread, where sharp upright
In starlight stood the stones

Of Machrie Moor, a sacred space
Where druids once paid service
To maidens of an ancyent race
In sacrificial bliss.

For Arran is a magic isle
For anyone who knows,
Where Danaan princes cairns did pile
Consecrating heroes.

'Goodbye my island,' Wullie sigh'd,
His whisperings disband,
The very moment that he died
In the middle of No Man's Land.

THE GOLGOG OF GLEN ROSA

Old Malakai pick'd up a knife
& stuck his *'fucking boring wife,'*
Then drove around & park'd the car
& acted normal in a bar.

He drain'd his glass, he stepp'd outside,
The sea had wash'd up with the tide,
He thought at first to wade within
& cleanse his life of guilt & sin.

He threw, instead, his phone into
Those murky waters, then he drew
All of his wages from the bank,
For seven days just drank & drank.

His wife's young brother call'd & call'd,
Persistence pains, excuses stall'd,
"I'm coming down tomorrow, man,"
Old Malakai conjur'd a plan,

He'd leave forever Milton Keynes;
A jumper, coat, a pair of jeans,
A t-shirt & a paperback,
Was all his life was, in a sack.

He caught a train to London Town,
The police search'd for him up & down,
He shaved his beard & wore a hat,
Then chang'd his name & found a flat.

He dared not work, nor too far go,
With money on a one-way flow,
It dwindl'd in a dire descent,
Until he could not pay the rent.

Without a hope, without a name,
The killer's curse a face of fame,
So, off he wander'd to the wild
Of Scotland where the mountains piled.

He found a glen, he built a camp,
The summer short, the autumn damp,
The winter cold, spring barely better,
Wilder, windier & wetter,

Where he will wander all year round,
Still fidgety at every sound,
His hat is torn, his beard is black,
& sometimes, weird, along the track,

He shuffles past the tourists, who
Will look a bit like me & you,
You'll know him by his lary look,
A monster in a scary book,

That stares at you without a wink,
& as you smell his dreadful stink,
Please, hurry past, no don't engage,
Else loose that killer from his cage.

For killers kill until they're caught,
He'll clamp his hands around your throat
& squeeze until your breath is gone,
Another dead, another one

Has vanish'd in the forest slutch;
A Swede, a German, & a Dutch,
A Fifer from Dalgety Bay,
Don't be the next one he 'gan slay.

Yes, hurry past, avert your eyes,
For contact makes his fevers rise,
& never slouch a wee look back
For he'll be crouching on the track,

Drooling at you with sneer'd intent,
A predator whose caught the scent,
Stood waiting for the trigger-glance,
No don't look back, this is your chance!

Escape, escape, get out the glen,
Catch ferries back, go home & then
Old Malakai push from your mind,
You've left that bastard far behind;

Where, mentally he's masticating
Flesh, & later masturbating,
Over bones where you & me
Might pass into posterity.

Aggravating, agitating,
Malakai stands salivating,
Thro' the skull-bone of your head
Drills bulging eyes of bloodshot red.

He's waiting for your face to turn,
With eyes that bleed, with eyes that burn,
The pull is fierce, the urge is strong,
A thousand thoughts about us throng.

But don't look back, what e'er you do,
I know you're really wanting to,
He could be coming now, you think,
Is that his breath upon the brink?

Are those his feet that closer thud?
Are you about to bleed your blood
Within this glen of shallow graves,
Of screams & chases, rapes & caves,

Where Malakai is now Golgog,
The grunt of boar, the face of frog,
The deathless Arran Al-Sameri,
Tortur'd by eternal, dreary

Fate eternal outcasts share,
Like Buttadeus, unaware
Offended Heaven, for all time,
Condemns him to repeat this crime.

So, Syracuse to Zaragoza,
Never venture to Glen Rosa,
Malakai seeks murders new,
He's kill'd his wife, now he'll kill you!

THE BATTLE OF CHESTER

Men fought a battle long ago
Aslant Pendragon skies;
Two armies met in weather wet,
Black crows crowded the skies.

Druids gather, stone circles glow,
Cast was a cryptic rune,
"The time is nigh, a king shall die
            Beneath a mystic moon!"

Dawn's glory shone, the Saxons rose
With sword & spear & shield,
Across the plain, in driving rain,
Old Cymry block'd the field.

For some it was a blushing morn,
Yet others fear'd the light;
Weapons glisten, two lines listen
For horns to launch the fight.

As flash-on-flash the weapons clash
Behind the crashing fray,
With smoke & bells the druid spells
Melt minds to disarray.

The Welsh are driven to their camps,
The sunset bled wound red,
The Saxons bring back to their king
Each sever'd foeman's head.

For every head a stone was found,
& there a barrow built,
Into the mound with shrieking sound
Men plunge long swords full hilt.

The next day dawn'd, its beauty lost,
The gods of battle reign,
The air grew still, fog left the hill,
& settled on the plain.

Two armies stood there paralyz'd,
Three bees buzz'd on the hush,
With startling cry, with swords held high,
Men made an angry rush.

As flash-on-flash the weapons clash
Behind the crashing fray,
With smoke & bells the druid spells
Melt minds to disarray.

The music of the battle rang
Cross country shore-to-shore,
A legend born, no-one had known
How cruel could be war.

As kings & princes, fathers, sons
Commingl'd for the fray,
Death dips & darts, for many hearts
This was their final day.

Death after death, duel after duel,
The Saxons press their might,
'Til at the line, 'midst forest pine,
Two princes met to fight.

Aethefrith's son is Looe the strong,
Selyf bore Slainge the fair,
A lethal fray, & to this day
Looe's bones are buried there.

As flash-on-flash the weapons clash
Behind the crashing fray,
With smoke & bells the druid spells
Melt minds to disarray.

King Selyf led them from the front,
This day the land's held fate,
T'was life & death, with striving breath
They held the Roman gate.

The Cymric King is set upon,
Three javelins pierc'd his side,
He slew all three by the wind-blast tree,
& then lay down & died.

Slainge dropp'd his spear & paced alone
Before the Saxon band,
He met the king, & slid his ring
Upon his handsome hand.

His father buried neath the field,
His battle cairn grew high,
So many stones, so many bones,
Might Selyf reach the sky?

So, if you find yourself one night
Aslant Pendragon skies,
Come cast a rune, sing to the moon,
& watch the spirits rise.

THE BALLAD OF PENDLE HILL

Auld Pendle Hill standest alone
Twyx fortress Clitheroe
& Burnley vale, heart of a tale
The World shall come to know.

She broods deep in the misty North,
So sheer & solemn piled,
Midst hoar & spacious moorland wastes,
& woodlands thick & wild.

Auld Pendle is a savage place,
Sabden to Barley Fold,
Of rushing rills & rolling hills
& damp, north-facing mould.

Where mist sets thick, where elf-lights trick
The mind at every turn,
When in winds wild sometimes a child
Will never home return.

Auld Pendle is a misty place
Beneath her whale back sheer,
Where dissipation saturates
At all times of the year.

Wide-scatter'd all about her rim
Lie villages & farms;
Whose folk, in gales, huddle round tales
Of curses, spells & charms.

Aye, this is where the Boggart dwells
To feed on living souls,
To pounce & prey on those who stray
Too close to hidden holes.

Where, sixteen epic centuries
Since Jesus' final hour,
A coven stands all holding hands,
In Malkin's blackest tower.

By candlelight old Demdike stood,
Some prophet in the sands,
"Sisters", she said, *"we daemon-wed*
Do what the Beast commands!"

They sacrific'd a stolen sheep,
They drank its boiling blood,
Smearing crimson wyrdly upon
Bare breasts, as witches should.

From arcane tongue a ghastly song
All thunder'd to the deep,
To touch the ear of something queer,
That rous'd it from its sleep.

Across the coven's cavern floor,
Crones chalk white pentacles,
Twyx ancient runes & crescent moons
Crawl slimy tentacles...

Auld Pendle is a wild, wild place
There wolves, there, growl & croon,
Where by the cats the long-nosed bats
Inspiral by the moon.

Then, if you ever pause to view
That Pennine climbing high
On Halloween, count to thirteen,
& then ye'll hear a cry

Of women wailing through the night
On broomsticks round the hill,
When ye shall swear, up from her lair,
Old Demdike cackles still.

SONNETS

MODERN LIFE

At this stage of Mankind's *devolution*,
We live in an age of air pollution,
Fat-cats & taxes, taxi fares, faxes,
Serial killers, silky leg waxes,
Condoms, modems, gimmicks, gadgets, gizmos,
Two rubber ducks & comic book heroes,
Football... rock & roll... catwalk... movie stars,
Recession, depression & wonder bras,
Four packs & prozac, pylon countryside,
Anarchist daughter, schoolboy suicide,
Just-add-water, slaughter of Mother Earth,
Demise of religion, pagan rebirth,
Not one inch left of this globe to explore,
The whole world itchin' for its third World War!

THIS IS MY COUNTRY

Good Morning Great Britain
Still great, still Britain
The sun is shining, 10:45 AM
£296.26 pence in my pocket
Time to bet it all on black & hit the road again

If time is a mere scratch & life is nothing
& nothing that occurs of the slightest importance

Aberdeen to Birmingham, Arundel & Deal
Dullis Hill to Rotherham, Bristol & Peel
Inverness to Liverpool, Leeds & Palmer's Green
Lewisham to Padiham & all the pubs between
Badminton to Twickenham & Barton-in-the-Beans

'Til my bardic breath expires

This is my Time
        This is my Rhyme
                This is my Country

WESTENDERS

Twas a quintessential English evening,
All about town & the capital's core,
On my arm a wonderful flutterling,
Perfectly amenable to the tour.

We met in a wine-bar off Trafalgar,
To delve within a cozy eaterie,
Then took our places at the theater
For the Mousetrap's befuddling mystery.

O! The night brimm'd a goblet romantic,
& our spirits, yes, they sparkl'd as the stars;
Rosie was a gentle alcoholic,
Floating, flirting, thro' her favorite bars;

When, to the chimes
            Of Big Ben's booming bells,
We jump'd the last train down
            To Tunbridge Wells...

ROSIE'S SCHOOL RUN

OH MY GOD! I'm having a nightmare,
Fuck, look at the fucking time!
"SHUUTTT UUUPPP!!!"
The kids are doin' my head in
With their school-stuff everywhere,
"Here's yer shoes, here's yer socks,
Heres yer fuckin' sandwich box!"
"MUMMY... don't swear!"
OH MY GOD! Its ten to nine now,
& my car-keys JUST AREN'T THERE!

Will it rain? Will mum call?
Will I end up on the dole?
O MY GOD! Its five to nine now
& the traffic's hit a WALL!

TRAINING IN THE ART OF FARE EVASION
The Fader Code

1: Remain alert
2: Always keep your cool
3: Trust your instincts
4: Never show your money
5: Know your stations
6: Another five minutes won't hurt in the loo
7: Know your enemy
8: Know your postcodes
9: The train's going there anyway
10: When in doubt, clout
11: Trains always comes when ya skinnin' up
12: It is every Fader's duty to baffle & confuse
13: Always remember your free cup of tea
14: No need to rush unless you're being chas'd

RECOLLECTIONS: FIRST KISS
Partridge Walk, Burnley

I was a six-year-child when first I felt
My soul entwining with the fairer sex,
Em'rald-eyed neighbor, who, one starry night
Said, *"Have you ever kiss'd a lass before?"*
"Of course!" I yelp'd, but grandmas do not count,
& as we kiss'd she giggled at my lips
Closed shut & clamp'd by frigid innocence,
& said, *"No, not like that, ya kiss like this!"*
& show'd me how my mouth should act a fish.

Soon sprinting home, embarrass'd at the deed,
That never was repeated I believe,
For looking back, I was, in tender days,
Contented with the kisses of grandmas,
& nee-owwwwing with little Corgi Cars.

MI' DAD

Yes, I'm really glad yer mi dad, Dad,
Yer the best that a young lad could have, Dad,
Yer better than that bloomin' Sir Galahad,
Yer mi dad, Dad!

Aye, I'm really glad I'm yer lad, Dad,
Cos I get to crash in yer pad, Dad,
& chat to yer when I'm all sad, Dad,
Yer mi dad, Dad!

Yer always so bloody well clad, Dad,
& make the best eggs that I've had, Dad,
But yer brews, bloody 'ell, they're so bad, Dad,
Yer mi dad, Dad!

& better still, yer mi mate, mate,
& I love yer, an that's fuckin' great!

SKYE

As Kestrels surf the mountain-fringed spaces,
Road twists between saturnine gargants,
Romantic mounds of monstrous magma,
Marvelous Munros of aulden minstrel-song,
Lost in the moment, eyes keen to the skies,
Hard traveling unravels, sailing above us
Silver-fire mists of the sylvan alpine rise,
& beyond, entering the stunning scope
Of another planet, another Jupiter,
Sodden expanse of treeless waste,
But beautiful land, stupendous Cuillin hills,
Seats of Titans, where thrusting solar shafts
Induce startling notions of timelessness –
Here there is no time,
                    Only milky flowing waterfalls.

A DAY IN THE LIFE OF LOVE

We talk'd last night
&, after we made love,
I read to you the Lao-Tse Tung;

In my voice rose ancyent chimes,
Funell'd thro' the Jiayuguan Pass
In elegant simplicity –
Lass, after we made love, I cherish'd thee!

Night comes again,
The drift of day deserts us,
The dusk is all that matters now, my love;
The light is dimming,
                    But thine eyes are bright,
As, cradl'd in these arms,
You smile to me once more -

Love, let us talk again.

EDINBURGH ZOO

When Noah's Ark left two-by-two,
They'd hurry back in if they'd knew
They'd one day end up in a zoo
For all the fucking world to view;
The Wolverine, the Kangaroo,
The Lesser Spiral-Horn'd Kudu,
The Chimpanzees in pirate crew,
The Turacoo of violet hue,
The coarse-quill'd, stiff-claw'd, casque Emu,
Flies flocking to the Rhino poo,
The Pygmy Hippo, &, what's new,
The Ocellated Turkey too!
 Barbaric as the Human herds,
        An Alcatraz of Beasts & Birds!

VAGABONDO

Solo, sono stato viaggio,
Dalle complessita senza vita,
Di villagio in villaggio,
Panarami di vista a vista –
Oh! sospiri di Viareggio,
Oh! Gatti schelectrici di Calcata,
Solo, sono stato viaggio,
Dalle complessita senza vita.

Stelle quando sono campeggio,
Pensiero sul passagio,
Oh! isola balena di Ponza,
Oh! comode piazza,
Oh! di Portovenere bellezza,
Oh! simplice mezza-vita!

*Alone, I was a journey, from complexities without
life, from village to village, panoramas from view
to view – O! sighs of Viareggio, O! skeletal cats of
Calcata, Alone, I went wandering, from
complexities without life. Stars when I am
camping, thoughts upon the path, O! whale-island
of Ponza, O! comfortable city-squares, O! beauty
of Portovenere, O! uncomplicated half-life!*

HELL'S GATES

THRO ME THE WAY INTO THE WOEFUL CITY
THRO ME THE WAY TO THE ETERNAL PAIN
THRO ME THE WAY AMONG
THE LOST PEOPLE
ABANDON ALL HOPE
THOSE THAT ENTER HERE

Holding breath I enter a starless gloom,
Sounds like whirlwind-eddying sand
surround my head,

Clapping hands,   * Screams of anguish
Haunted sighs * Lamentations
Loud Wailings * Strange Tongues
Horrible Lingua * Words of Pain

The poet saw me shrink back from those
Angry tones & said,

"Welcome to the Inferno!"

Breathing deeply & holding my breath
I stepp'd into the land that men call Limbo...

BELOW SCOPELLO

To become, to belong, bohemian,
So many miles my smitten songsmith sent,
Striving for prospects paradesean,
In an immortal moment's monument –
Time carves us this vista Tyrennean,
Tranquilo corner of a continent,
To become, to belong, bohemian,
So many miles my smitten songsmith sent.

This rocky cove, this tower, this mountain,
Blend in an often prophesied fusion,
Sweet Sicily! Sate silent & content,
Recently have my dreams increasing seen
Visions of places I had never been,
Where I should sit a songsmith & invent.

CASTALIAN SPRING

So, this is the heartbeat of poetry,
From holy Parnassus, uprising sheer!
These pure, empyrean magi-waters,
Pulse down from such a theater of stone,
To pour, abed, the depths of my studies,
Where in a sketch I see gargoyle faces,
Perhaps by Hobhouse in Lord Byron's *'Life.'*
Who came up too, tasted this ancient spring,
Upon his very famous *'Pilgrimage,'*
While mine is ended here... I sup the mead,
Faint hint of minerals, revitalized,
I swear to all my Muses I shall be
A poet still, & if they ride with me

To England,

I shall build them temples there!

THE INCREDIBLE INDIA CODE

1 Book your tickets in advance
2 Separate your money sources
3 Never trust a tout
4 Keep tabs on yer tabs
5 If they say they're a masseuse – they're not
6 Murder all mosquitoes before bed
7 Never trust a fart
8 Anything is possible in India
9 Check your room thoroughly before leaving
10 Pick'd up stones scare off dogs & monkeys
11 Eat with your non-wiping hand
12 "I was an Indian in another life!"
13 Plenty of change for journeys
14 Ask five different people for directions

THE EAR CLEANER

Stepping out one golden Goan morning,
Drowsy with the sunken sun's adorning,
Content was I to be in nature's hand,
Soul-freshen'd as bare feet sunk into sand,

From out of nowhere stept a wizen'd man,
"Sahib! cleaning your hearing well I can!"
Shows Western praises in his little book,
Black blocks of wax from both my ears he took.

I shook the hand that scrubs my hearing clear,
Said fond farewells & watch'd him disappear
Round red & rugged hill flank'd by the view
Of Konkan coast careering into blue;

When first found I the profits of his fee
I'd never known how sweetly sounds the sea!

POVERTY & WEALTH

Two goddesses bicker about beauty,
Content to start a second Trojan war,
Srinava's wisdom thunders crore on crore,
"My Jyesthadevi, my Laksmidevi,
There is a young carpenter of Bundi
Who is so very honest to his core,"
Supreme goddesses stand soon at his door,
"Who is the most beautiful, she or me?"

Most humble cobbler thought a mortal while,
Then says, *"Laksmi most lovely on arriving,*
Yet Jyestha gorgeous more when she departs;"
This answer made each goddess equal smile,
& he – celestial wrath surviving –
Learns flattery woos e'en immortal hearts.

CREATION

As thro' Mumbai I took the rickshaw home,
A great prostrate cow seem'd to be dying,
Guts on the pavement where she was lying,
But no… close by, lay her hour-old daughter.

I watch'd the wee one make her falt'ring first
Steps in the world, like an ambitious teen,
Thro' her mother's dung, slippery & green,
Then in the hot noon felt an earthly thirst;

Went looking for something,
                              Nuzzling half-blind,
She suckles on her mother's rough larynx,
Who stands up, motionless as sandy sphinx,
&, with a lick, acknowledges her kind;

Who creeps now forwards to the golden teat
& clamps down hard
                              As angels swoop the street.

EPYLLIA

THE GRAND TOUR

It's the end of March & my rent is due,
But two life options lie open to me;
Break with a lover, her friendship, split thro,'
Or chain myself to the servility
Of capitalism... A poet true
I yearn to be, so young, so sure, so free;
Romancin' my mind with poetry's flow,
So be it, with sure brave heart, let me go.

I made love to my love the night before
I wrapp'd my guitar in a grey, baggy
Jumper once worn on cold nights down Turf Moor,
Raided the bank for all my rent money,
& embark'd upon a third busker's tour –
Her scent mull'd like wine, her tongue lull'd honey,
How we laugh'd as we revell'd, dear Rosie,
In kisses & love-songs & pure poesy!

I watch the white cliffs recede to a speck,
Then sang a fond farewell to old Blighty,
When, like a wreck-head at a discotheque,
A certain chunderness docks to smite me,
I had to head down to the under-deck,
Feeling so sick I think I should whitey –
As one voyage ends, another embarks
At Ostend, changing Pounds to Francs & Marks.

I take the greatest train jump of my tour
From Vienna to Villach, on a sleek
Inter-City, as each Alp towers o'er
My little carriage, each volcanic peak
Thrust from the fertile, verdant valley floor
With breathtakin' beauty – I could not speak,
Until dinnertime by a mountain stream...
Austria's watchers echo'd to my scream.

How glad am I to enter Italy,
For the call of the muse grows ever strong,
Like some wild animal trapp'd inside me,
To find fair form in my juvenile song;
Snowy mountains shrink to a flat country,
Thro' fields of lazy green we zoom'd along,
To Venice; as Italy greets my feet
A grand canal sparkles... but where's the street?

Three days I spend in ardor Venetian,
Three nights in a disused railway carriage,
Gusting around this floating museum
On life's perfect barge; there is a marriage
Between my soul & the elysian,
A poet's dreams come pulsing to the page,
As here in this soft city I savor
My first Italian ice cream flavor!

Distant Riviera di Levante
My heart's destination, mine art's true call,
But first, the mausoleum of Dante,
To tap into a predecessor soul,
Overgrown with moss & creeping ivy,
My man, you were the wildest of us all!
Ravenna, this may be a swift sojourn,
But one day, with my wife, I shall return.

How balmy is the Florentine evening,
Whose stylish sweetness softens Dante's tongue,
Outside Shelley's old villa I'm busking,
To soon attract a most beautiful throng
Of German frauleins young, & visiting
This sultry city, entranc'd by my song,
Two of them follow me into a park
For passionate encounters in the dark.

We wake in arms! After cappuccinos,
We wander moped streets, a sacred city
Thro' which argent-sheen'd Arno slowly flows;
I buy a book to fill with poetry,
On the title page Maya draws a rose,
Then buy fresh foods & climb a hill where we
Build a fire, cook dinner, watch the sunshine
Fade over Florence with a sweet red wine.

'How romantic it is to be abroad,
Free from the chains of a working mans day,'
Think I while walkin' the main Pisan road
Passing a troupe of buskers on the way
With guitar, ink-pens & notebook my load
I've arrived, & all my dreams fade away
Seeing the leaning tower – am I drunk?
On further inspection one side has sunk.

Back from the tower *Fate* bids me to meet
The busker's troupe in musical mid-flow;
There's an old black bluesman with dust-bare feet,
A dark, Chilean named Kapitano,
Then a saxman sultrifying the street;
They offer me wine, adding my oestro,
You've never heard a more raunchier noise,
& just like that! I'm one of the bad boys.

I settle with this best of holidays;
Each one begins with pasta from a nun,
Then idle hours spent musing under rays
Of an English summer-like springtime sun;
When falls the warm evening I, then, amaze
The Pisan public with songs sweetly spun,
& blitzed on six bottles of Tuscan red,
Outside a church we make our cardboard bed.

I jump a train to San Guilliano,
To walk on Shelley's mountains, but, instead,
I'll sit in the street with old man Franco,
He ploughs me with red, risotto & bread,
Plus a whole sow's leg – my stomach doth blow!
Tho' we hardly understand a word said,
Conversazione; war, England, life,
Italy, poetry & his dead wife.

I wander up the coastline for to muse,
Setting up camp in a cliffside quarry,
Resplendent in luscious blue sea-side views;
By the chapel of Portovenere,
Tonight, my life, my mind, mine art shall fuse,
&, awakening to my destiny,
Prepare for the sun to set 'low the line,
By buildin' fire, ent'rin town, stealin' wine.

With topless bottle of red in my hand,
I scamper up cliff face with the surge-might
Of some fabl'd hero from Plato's land,
When, claiming the top, gulls in freedom's flight,
Silhouetted setting sun, a wide band
Of gold spread 'cross azure seas, from this height
I muse upon rippling sea-meadows blue –
This evening gives birth to a poet true.

I pause to reflect on the life I knew;
Nice house, nice job, nice girl, nice skunk, nice deal;
Compare these to these skies & seas of blue,
And this sense of sheer assurance I feel
At joinin' the bravestars, we happy few –
No more a cog on the soul-grindin' wheel,
Besides, England does my fuckin' brain in,
& I bet, as I'm writin,' it's rainin'.

Dizzying to my heart's epiphany,
The last sun-chink was slipping 'low the line,
Her deep shed ray sped 'cross the darkling sea
To sparkle on an object, close, divine;
A Silver Rose, so lovely & so wee,
Had caught my eyes, drunk on delightful shine,
I pluck'd my moment's floral memento,
Then left for camp, led by its lamp-like glow.

Southwards I go, to Viareggio,
Beside the Apennines, whose lofty height
Towers o'er the lines of my fine canto,
As shrouded by the drowsy, star-strewn night,
I build a fire beside the softsea flow,
Cook up a meal, by fading ember light
I shed a tear for some long-ago year,
When Shelley's corpse was found & burnt
                                        Right here!

Soon I am back in bohemian swing
Musing away; one long, mellow daydream;
By the side of the Arno sometimes sing,
Or bask in the sun with wine & ice-cream,
Or busk to the world as a poet-king,
Then party hard with Kapitano's team;
For life is forever tender to me
Having tasted the breath of Italy.

In the warm morning, after a party,
I sit with Kapitano round a fire;
He teaches me the bird-songs of Chile
& how to busk a day without a lyre;
Brimming with wisdom into the city
I drift, when, in a shock of love desire,
She's sat on the grass, banging wee bongos,
'...*to describe the way I feel*,' the song goes.

She seems to me the first fair star of Eve,
With ocean eyes & smile of teeth pearl white,
And perfect curves like you wouldn't believe,
My heart melteth at the sensual sight
Of beauty's first essence, this I receive
In raptures, as we, by the Arno's flight,
Converge as one 'til comes the sad sundown –
'*Meet me in Rome*,' we kiss & she leaves town.

Heading down south on the click-clack train track,
At two AM the conductor finds me
With a bag of books, the rags on my back,
& in my hands a copy of Shelley;
Expecting some Hampshire inspector's flak,
The guy, instead, showers me with pity –
Six hours later, the twilight before dawn,
I walk the streets of Rome waiting for morn.

I jump a tram this sunniest of days
Down into the tourist-laden city,
Upon the Spanish Steps I pause & laze
Then walk into a shrine of poetry;
It is true the true poet seldom pays,
Reciting a passage from my Shelley,
I get in for free, see hand at first hand,
For this & this only I'll make my stand!

I sharpen my features & dress to impress,
Enter, by candlelit, the theatre,
Where dark, Grecian drama's in deep progress,
Aha! There's my marvelous Manuela,
My sexy, smilin', stage-struttin' actress,
I knew right then that I had to have her,
"You look beautiful, like a Silver Rose!"
That night… her hotel floor… our teeth-torn clothes.

With my lady sleepin', thro' the city,
I roam, dawning sun illumines the streets,
A peaceful Protestant cemetery,
& Shelley's tower, where my Muse completes
Her visitation; left me tired, empty,
But wait! As I stood by the grave of Keats
I surge with strength to try the train-jump home,
& did one from the glory that was Rome.

I pass thro' Pisa, glance at the Arno,
Chancing trains to an uncertain future,
Then once again view'd Viareggio,
Le Spezia, as, beyond Genoa,
Sunset spent in the streets of Torino,
There skipp'd on a train to the French border –
But travelin' don't always go to plan,
I'd fuck'd up & upended in Milan!

I was now sev'ral hundred miles of course,
& how it happen'd did not understand,
But youth is driven by a hidden force,
Which made me jump a train to Switzerland,
At whose harsh border found I smart resource –
For they had me rejected out of hand
(I look'd like a tramp) – after midnight, tense,
I found a wee rabbit-hole in the fence.

I felt like I'd escaped Colditz Castle,
But as I pass'd thro' chocolate Zurich,
I was toss'd into a world of hassle,
The Swiss care not for buskers & their reek;
After lots of shouting & a wrestle,
I was plung'd in a police cell for my cheek,
But come sundown everything was sorted –
The next day I was to be deported!

They marched me on a fancy Swiss Air Jet,
Handcuff'd until the very last moment,
For I had slipped right thro' their border net,
Back to my native island must be sent,
On fine French wine my flight was free from fret,
For thanks to their filthy rich government –
I carried massive bundles of Swiss Francs,
The dowry of their Nazi-lovin' banks.

I thrill'd so much to drop down to Heathrow,
Tho' from the wine a little worse for wear,
To Rosie's boudoir hopefully I'll go –
At first she gives me such a startl'd stare,
But soon romancing reconvenes its flow,
& fed her verses on a velvet air,
Said she, *"Why don't we take a bath, my sweet…"*
With that hot wash this Grand Tour was complete.

SQUATTING LONDON

Thro' neon night & raucous roads,
A credit to style & the words on the street;
GUITARS DESTROY KNICKER ELASTIC!
We hit Brixton Hill & the King of Sardinia,
Aging pub taken over by even older hippies,
Urban refuge for madmen & rejects;
My man Jimmy Van de Mere shows up,
I strutted with him down into Brixton,
Discussing life, & the fact that I'm homeless,
He gives me the shpiel of a property just open'd,
"Bastards made it squatter proof, s'yours mate…"
I'm just arriving as he is sick of London,
"Haven't heard anything original for fiv,e years!"

Then let it begin
The greatest rock n roll show
Since Hendrix came to town
With a bag full of uppers, downers & all overs

The pills arrive with the Bognor crew,
Coke in the loo & handfuls of shrooms,
Classic acid to enhance the vibe,
Shady promoter skulks in the background,
Counting his cash with a glint in his eye;
The audience was ready as I took to the stage,
Lights so bright I couldn't see the crowd,
Blasting thro' tunes, back to front, top to bottom,

Strings melted to hand, fingers on easy groove,
Pepperland panache on an Entwistle roll,
Moments on stage like you'd never believe,
Psychic conversations & electric orgasms
Of a rock n roll nirvana… & then it was over
The birds came over as I merg'd with the crowd,
"Best band I've seen in years," said the manager,
Everyone's high on the drugs & the music,
Like rough-cut diamonds we shine with the stars.

A girl I gave some shrooms to sidles over,
"Fancy a smoke?" That's what I call karma;
We leave the venue for the psychedelic night,
She's an artist… Poets & Painters,
"Boets & Bainters," said King George the First,
Sat in a post gig glow she cooks up some chi,
Smoking the skunk in her funky kitchen,
Fit as fuck in an unkempt kinda way.

I love her to pieces!
I love the way she plays seventies classics
On a clarsach harp -
It gave me a hard on,
A musical hard on, that is.

 We chat about life, drugs & music
"Wanna do some art!*"* she offers, *"alright babe!"*
She strips off her clothes, flips to hot pose,
I started to sketch her & thought, *'what the hell*

Am I drawin' her for,' & neatly suggested
A congress of the tiger, the cat or the deer.

Next day, detoxing on antioxidant,
Jimmy took me down to Clapham Junction;
Everyone passes thru here at some stage,
As I do today, not to see, but to stay -
In my house, perched on Dorothy Road
Alright, there's no gas or electricity,
Water or modern-day accoutrements -
But four hundred grand worth of property
Can't be sniffed at... he shook my hand
& skipped up the road...

    ...I got my bearings:
Battersea library at the top of my street,
Full of books & a grand old cinema for the footy,
Free calls on the phones down at the job center,
The spacious common just stone's throw away,
I love my Bohemian paradise!
& Clapham is proper up & coming;
A cultural center, cool bars & the theaters,
Where Tuesday nights are 'pay-what-you-can,'
A pound a play at the Latchmere & BAC,
&, on the road betwixt them,
A swimming pool with a slack front desk,
Free showers & a swim for whenever I want.

I turn'd the key, & entered rent free,
A tall stately home, like some cool caravan,
Put up my section six in the window,
Five grand fine or a few months in the nick
To anyone who tries to move me on;
Reliques of an artist clog the attic,
Soon decorating my wholesome abode,
Furnished by the streets & the Oasis shop,
Transported my bed in pieces on the busses,
No television to rot & shape my brain,
Just the snap & crackle of an open fire,
& Classic FM from a cheap shower radio,
&, when I want to leave my Bohemian paradise,
Just flash an old ticket to fly on the busses
Or jump on a train at the scurrying junction.

I have me a shave for a stroll round the town,
A poet's night out, those random & aimless
Saunters thro' cities which always roll good,
"Could you spend a day with no money at all
& still eat well & feel thoroughly entertain'd?"

I found myself at the Queen Elizabeth Hall,
Perched by the river in all it's civic splendor,
Milling with punters — it must be the interval
I slip in amongst them, flow free to the music
(well would you buy a half-eaten sandwich);
Bert Jansch is having his 60th birthday
Picking so haunting, chaunting half-spoken,

Sound stylishly sandwich'd
By Bernard Butler & Jonny Marr,
The applause is astounding,
                    I leave the building...

I hop on a bus,
Little fuss,
My brain
Pretends to be elsewhere,
The few passengers
Watch me sit
A black woman
A young punk
Old man twiddles his tash

A young girl studies the Victorian Age;
I mention she should read Christina Rossetti,
Her mother says, *"Oh yes, she was a poet wasn't
she?"*
I agree as the bus climaxes at the Junction
& off I will wander, breath mist in the air.

There is a song the Stone Roses used to sing,
      About Paris & the '68 student uprising,
I hum it to myself as the night grows crisper,
 Victorian terraces turning off their televisions
      As I turned the key, & enter rent free
            Repasting in my castle for the first time...

THE HONEYMOON

Sundrunk & tipsy, skies beryl with lace,
Waves mulberry porcelain, with a twirl
Emerges Sally; body, legs & face
Dripping with sea-droplets, each a pearl;
Love forges as one, elsewhere from this place,
A breathless moment as I seize my girl
& squeeze her tight, with one stern kiss demand,
A look of love from Sally, on the sand.

My Pisan streets, how I return to thee,
This time a wife fix'd sweetly by my side,
That like a Muse comes merrily to me,
Or is she you, who gaylie deified
My youthful verse, when wed to poetry,
Ye urged me on the world to wander wide,
From Tuscan marriage; girl, I sense ye still,
About my mind, my woman & my will.

Thro' shabby-chic, electric hub-hub, wheel
Our feet to some fallen Contessa's suite,
A casa with an antiquated feel,
With books & art & beds above the street;
This is a shrine where all past heartaches heal,
In all this blissful happiness & heat,
Where, dressing well, we, hand-in-hand, go out –
Pure love has bless'd us Sally, there's no doubt.

We dine in narrow streets where market cart
Goes clunking thro' still tables' laziness,
With tender hand-strokes rarely far apart
We savor flavors with a shared finesse,
'Thou votary of Venus that thou art,'
Sing I, *'let us commence our coziness...'*
Sally's eyes, with candor unremitting,
Agreed to leave the seats where we were sitting.

As pleasure is a pleasurable thing,
& love atween two lovers yon reproach,
When, into evening, crickets sit & sing,
Our lips are warm, two moths about the torch,
With passions flashing on a febrile wing,
Her blushes fiery flushes in the scorch,
She yields that look, tho' words were never said,
'My Love, let us get naked, & abed!'

Sally, fashionista of the Bon Ton,
Undresses like a Duchess by the sedge
Of some brook's forest bank; *'Until Heaven*
Finds a better sky,' say I, *'my love's pledge*
Is yours,' with sultanas' wept devotion,
She smiles, sits down upon the quilted edge,
Patting down level space for us to be
Flesh unified in breathless ecstasy.

With ribbons pink I hook'd her to the mesh
Of iron at the bedcrown; scarlet silk
Sheets aswathe naked skin, a Marakesh
Of tingling tongue-tips, spirits springing milk,
Her arching back, her tightenings of flesh,
The breeze of freedom; I, strong-antler'd elk
Above the glen her smooth, moist body made,
Where glisten sweatdrops in an elfen glade.

We slept, lock'd tight like gorse bush, limbs in limbs,
Then awoke in the contented glory
That love's truth breeds; *'like cucumber with pimms,*
We just work, dear Sally, mia amore;
Here in this land of artistry & hymns,
Where love & heart rhyme – heart is cuore –
& poet's minds must focus on one thing...
His Muse who taught the Goddess Moon to sing!'

With vocab well-rehearsed I testify
'Mia moglie e imbarazzato,'
I noticed Giovanni's narrowed eye,
'L'ultima notte ha commenciato
Sua mestruazione,' paused I
For effect, a timely *'inatesso,'*
&, *'adesso c'e sonno macchia*
Sulla lenzuale,' all sung calm & clear.

Paris, we love you, we do already!
More kudos than any earthly city,
Wafts of an intoxicating, heady,
Melting of ethnic electricity,
Creates a certain soft, stoic, steady
Rapture for living life's felicity
Sense I, but think not, nor feel, as we march
Under the Arc de Triumph's varnish'd arch.

This busted land of sweet Lutetian airs,
Of charming boulevards & barges trim,
Of cinemas & parks, where, on green chairs,
Parisians thro' poet's pages skim,
Thy searing beauty caught us unawares,
Like infants hearing a first holy hymn,
When, most of all, we loved the way plann'd we
To spend a future holiday with thee.

Somewhere, in the Fifth Arrondissement,
Our hotel stands - with one of Longchamps' maps
Guiding our steps, we found the logement –
Hotel le Clos de Notre Dame – whose taps
Shone like seraphs; 'neath timber beams, sat on
The windowsill we peer'd between the gaps
Of blinds & curtains – faces, fabric, feet –
Some champagne chandelier above the street.

This is a place where people give a shit
About how looks their home, a fine antique
Reeking of stories,' *'Sally let us sit*
Awhile by Notre Dame,' there, cheek-to-cheek,
We cuddl'd, kissing in a perfect fit,
Souls sensing, *'c'est fluide et c'est complique,'*
When every single second comes too soon,
The joy & sadness of our Honeymoon.

Back in our chamber, touching skin, I find
Sally's panties' paradise, with a slant
I slip my hands between, a gentle grind,
'Til thrusting finger pays the gold bezant
& lust delays no longer, in a bind
Of bodies, breaking silence, with a pant,
Or, she a squeak, or I, the sunken gasp
Of climax, bodies clamp'd as magnets clasp.

I've lived before, but now I'll live real life,
As pleasant as a summer morning stroll,
She's destiny, she's perfect, she's my wife,
The one thing that I can, & can't, control,
Who sometimes seems as sharp as shark-tooth knife,
Sometimes as tender as a suckling foal,
With she, the need to roam the world withstood,
Her heart my home, her happiness my blood.

CANTATA

SONG OF THE MORNING

The sky is pink, & rose, & red,
A chink of golden sun!
It's almost time to leave your bed,
The day has scarce begun.

Be glad for this beautiful morning!
Now that Dawn has deliver'd us day,
Go & shake off your sleep with a yawning,
To the whiff of a café au lait.

But, if the hours to roll ahead
Seem thorny, rough & steep,
Don't drag back up your duvet spread
To plunge off back to sleep.

No! what a precious stepping stone
This day of life ahead;
All yours, these hours, this life, alone,
So, mate, get out of bed!

The longest day's in June, they'll say,
The shortest in December,
Whatever day it is, today's
A day you'll long remember.

Wake up! Wake up! A sudden surge
Of energy arises,
This day's excursions will converge
On thrilling, bright surprises.

Wake up, get flex'd with yer stretches,
Or yoga if yer that way inclin'd,
In yer mind draw up plans & make sketches,
Days run better if cleverly design'd.

But, leave some spontaneous spaces,
& savor them, random & rife,
Meeting different people & places
Are the flavorsome spices of life.

For life is a wonder, enjoy it!
Let it's living be sweet & sublime,
Today let us leave a fine footprint
On the shores of the oceans of time.

Yes, it's time to escape from your bedding,
Pop on kettles & toasters & hobs,
& I know they might batter yer 'ead in,
But we've got to get on with our jobs!

They say each day's a novel bound,
But what kind could it be?
A history? A mystery?
We'll have to wait & see!

For there's rivers & there's rainbows,
There is savory, there is sweet,
There are children in the meadows
Chasing butterflies in bare feet.

Mate, it's no use feeling bitter,
& it's pointless getting mad,
& it's no good always longing
For the things we've never had.

A bell's not a bell to 'til you ring it,
A song's not a song 'til you sing it,
A friend's not a friend 'til you miss 'em,
A kiss is not real 'til you kiss 'em.

Today no folk ye shall offend,
Nor be yourself offended,
& what's amiss let's strive to mend,
There's nowt that can't be mended.

If feeling things just don't seem right,
Release the need to grouse,
To fret & gloom, from room-to-room,
 Sulk-stropping thro' the house.

If yesterday, when things got tough
& you gave up, said, *'that's enough,'*
A moan won't make life's fog less thick,
Its sunny smiles that do the trick!

Vow to yourself today's the day
When all your worries cease,
For hearts untouch'd by worrying
Are hearts at peace & ease.

With patient ear, with open eyes,
With ready, helping hand,
With gentle spirit & a heart
That's quick to understand,

Whate'er your goals & dreams you'll find
They can't be reach'd a glance behind -
Life's chances only e'er appear
For those who forwards thro' life steer.

With 'doing' let thy day be fill'd,
So many misconstrue,
We cannot reputations build
On what we're *going* to do.

& wouldn't days be drear & long
If all went right & nothing wrong,
O! what a world so dull & flat,
With not a jot there to grumble at.

There might be bullies in the schools,
Or mildew in the steeple,
But think of problems as the tools
To polish us as people.

If gloomy strains thy mind enshrouds,
Remembering stigmas you've fear'd
In former times, depressing clouds
Thro' actions fast disappear'd.

Open your mind to hope's soft sway,
From future worries part,
& let no mournful yesterday
Disturb thy peace of heart,

When it's better to apologize,
Nothing's gain'd from delay,
Left festering, your good intent,
Like all things, must decay.

'I'm sorry mate,' or *'love,'* or *'ma'am,'*
Costs nothing but yer pride,
Such simple message, soft & calm,
Shall soothe the storms inside.

Be prompt if friend or duty calls,
Be deaf to scandal's know-it-alls,
& if your faith has ebb'd away,
Stand up & reach for God today.

Have courage when facing your problems,
For none have e'er striven in vain,
& there never was glorious rainbow
Without a wee splatter of rain.

Those negative thoughts, they'll all have to go,
So, try & say *'yes,'* when you want to say *'no,'*
& never say, *'can't,'* saying only, *'I'll try,'*
Accepting things happen, not wonder,
                                    'but why?'

Then, mingling with this wondrous world,
By choice, or situation hurl'd,
One step won't take you very far,
You've got to keep on walking,
One word won't tell folk who you are,
You've got to keep on talking.

Perhaps you'll be fac'd with the violent,
With all of their moron attacks,
If so, take time out & be silent,
Switch off, run a bath & relax.

There refrain from complaining about it,
For gossip's a dangerous game,
When slateful words & idle talk,
Can harm the honest name.

A careless word might kindle strife,
A bitter word might hate instill,
A cruel word might wreck a life,
But gracious words might someone thrill!
So, do your work & do it well,
Let others gossip how they will!

Before you love somebody else,
You'll have to learn to love yourself,
Upon achievements set your sights,
& climb them to their highest heights.

Look out for ways to help our friends,
& better, even, strangers,
Encourage all to make amends,
& warn them if there's dangers.

If misfortune grumbles past ya,
Whatever, today, might befall,
Look, won't be a complete disaster,
For life carries on, after all.

If miff'd, don't leave the drift unsaid,
Relief lives in an emptied head,
Nor keep nice comments in the dark,
There's beauty in a kind remark.

If friends have gifts encourage them,
If faults, first recognise
The perfect time to mention them,
Lest friendships might capsize.

If there's a question left to solve
Somewhere within your heart,
All changes grow from firm resolve,
Such things must have a start.

When, climbing out of life's dark traps,
No matter how daunting the slope,
Tho' you spirits have sunk to your boot-straps,
& you feel that you simply can't cope;

Take a step, & then go take another,
Just a heave at a time, taking care,
With a flash of delight you'll discover,
One moment you're suddenly there!

& so, before you'll start your day
There's one last thing I'd like to say -
There's No need to huff & hurry,
Life is not all rush & worry,
For the world is full of magic
Take the time to stop & grasp it,
Catch the moment lest it dies,
Such enchantments can be fleeting,
Brief as passing butterflies!

SARASWATHI SONG

Bolivian hacendados plant the year's first coca,
Over Li Chiang, the snow range is turquoise,
As a stygian gloom clamps Krivarbatsky Lane,
Deadly fires devastate Stadhouderskade.

Josh sticks burn in Heliopolis,
Ginnungagap yawns,
Starlings gather in the pinetops,
Surya shines on an oily sea.

There are disturbances in the islands,
Iridescence has vanish'd from the morning,
There's a murders in the ruin'd agora,
There's a conflict in the churches of Aragon -
The twisted themes of tragic songs to come.

Atheism grows,
Poetry decays,
Life's lost passion slips from fashion;
But when one hears the call
Of Museworlds in conformity,
It leaves a single satisfactory sensation -
Be yourself, or nothing be,
& in that nothingness dissolve thy dreams.

Mortality escapes thro' ardent words,
&, if my mission not vain,
Let us excavate the kingdom by midsummer!

Bring me a versatile audience,
Lend me the tongue of King Shulgi of Ur,
Fill my breath with a storm of feeling;
We shall burn the incense to cinders,
We shall paint rabbits on the walls of tombs,
We shall blow the horn of Jerusalem,
Daubing lilies on the Temple's doors.

In the West my pen was chosen
By forces long forgotten,
Celebrating eloquence
Amang the risen bards,
When all my better parts
Churn in motion like the peasant's foot
Thro' forest wines in Avignon, fair made.

Do you remember the first time you found us,
Poeticizing in the caravanserai,
'Neath Tashkurghan's mountain Manchu fort,
& summon'd us to India, to sing
Thro' Saraswathi, Goddess of your land?

Into my mind, amassing,
Comes the debris of days
Trampl'd by time into chronicle dust,
Let alter egos spring from the divine!
Infuse in me the herbage of Ascelpius!
Pass me a dollop of pure opium,
A cup full of absinthe,
& a dream full of stars.

With motion-ness thro' passing youth,
I wander'd all across the lands
Of India, most useful -
O mighty huntress, & her prey, Mankind!

O Sarawasthi!
Time is auspicious, the venue appropriate;
As Sita with Rama, Damayanti with Nala,
Thro' due process of Svayamvara
Elect me as your husband, & I'll sing!

Our saliency is this, my sweet,
I am thy song disciple, let me sing!
Of being glimmering Skamandros,
& you, shimmering Xanthus,
A single river known by separate names.

Majestic Maharani of my mind!
If my passion-throng reciprocate,
Expanding like the petals of cut flowers
Teach me to weave webs of golden thread
& fill these soft stanzettas with your song,
In half-a-dream, or more a dream of dreaming.

Give me the lyrics of Mewari shepherds
Sate in fields of pristine sugar beets,
Slurping on stumps in between verses;
Give me melodies of Moslem bangle-sellers
Bustling thro' narrow alleyways of Hyderabad,
Where wedding chaunts of winking grooms,
Floral-wreath'd & crown'd like peacocks,
Handsome as the Dawn of Krishna's vows.

Sing, Saraswathi, of the Tyger of Mysore,
Stuck like a leg of chicken
In the British Empire's throat.

Let us hunt down the sloths of academia,
Inside the desolate, rockscapes of Balochistan,
Where desert-weather'd Sphinx,
& symmetrical Gopura,
Descry a deeper history than theirs

Teach me, O teach me,
Of the Ayer Vedic ghats,
Of the Edicts of Ashoka,
& the chains of causation,
Of ineffable contemplation
& these Four Noble Truths
First glean'd under the Bodhi Tree at Gaya.

The poets are cherish'd in Tibet,
Their richly respected Training & Tradition
Channel'd thro' changeless vocations of verse.

Sanskrit songs of elaborate measures,
Archaic spelling conjures ancient sages,
Concentric circles,
Poems of multiple directions.

Sing, Saraswathi,
Your tender, primal melodies,
For the girlfriends who ador'd me,
For the friends who did applaud me
& the women who once wash'd me,
When I was just a baby
In a far-off Burnley clime.

Sing, Saraswathi, of the golden Goan shoreline,
& the Kanchenjonga ridges
Oer the snake-streets of Sikkim.

Let us praise language in its highest form,
Most plainly & most openly,
My heroine is Truth,
I'll remain thy crystal paragon,
Adoring, with all aspects of my soul,
Who is, who was, & who shall be, always,
Most beautiful of all thy parts, my love.

Beyond senses, mind;
Beyond mind, reason;
Beyond reason, spirit;
Beyond spirit, Universe;
Beyond Universe – evolver of all things,
Precious Perusha pervades.

Sing, Saraswathi, of sacred Asvaghosha
& Ishavara Krishna of the Samkhyakarika,
How them both were Issa, as you've told me,
How Jesus of Judea was your prince!
Spreading Vedic principles
In texts of many tongues!

Saraswathi's untranslatable soul
Overflows with delicious association,
Sonorous verbal mist,
Spreading mind music;
Praise the sciences of embellishment,
Meditate on the making of magical metaphors,
Allow one word to do the work of twenty.

Her qualities are Nymphaeaceae,
Her perfumes Kustrika when on heat,
Bestowing immortality & the triumph of time!

But, Goddess, am I worthy ?
I am thy willing disciple,
My wildly discarnating spirit
Tameable with verses,
Of sacred diligence & reflections
Upon the perfection of the Puranas.

Traveling is difficult, traveling is hard,
Crossroads multiply like fractals,
But to fish the mind oriental,
Deliver its taste to desensitiz'd Occidentals,
Be the bright poet of divine proliferation,
I must wander on, & in my wanders wonder.

Unloosen all the ties which bind my heart!
Dismiss dreadful pathological misperceptions!
Burrow me with avenues of escape
From all this vintage monotony,
From all this village misogyny,
From all these weary desert sands
Of dead & dreary habits -
I am the magenta-throated,
Amethyst woodstar,
I am the pump of village water-wells,
I am the small dog digging holes in sand,
I am the hammer & sickle & Stalin's wall,
I am the secret street-cleaner at Dawn,
I am the calisthenics
Of an overweight agony aunt,
I am the aluminum rooves
Of barbers in Manilla,
I am the... everything!

Purusha is beyond definition,
To know Purusha is to understand
Liberation from mortality,
When only purest heart & purest soul,
Might sense, but never see, infinity!

O Saraswsathi!
Where Himalayas rise like Heaven,
Consummation falls in fragrances,
Condensing, on action, unimpeded intent

Dog-rough steeds need horse-taming Trojans!
Tropical inventions lie under ice!
Upon feet divinely guided, own'd by fate,
When amaranth pawns become pure Queens.

Let me praise thee with my thought,
Add music to the rivers of your righteousness,
In atmospheres of happiness & abundance,
A living poet & a bidden bard.

O Saraswathi!
Am I Kali, sworn to slay Asura?
Tell me in the spinning of a web,
Tell me in the shedding of the fleece,
Tell me in the crystal of your quartz,
Tell me in the Gita you gave to azure Krishna,
In the fields of Kurukshetra,
When Arjuna knew his doubts.

To the strains of your astral sitar,
Let us do what is to be done,
Gilded with erudite adamant,
Sail arks of gorgeous impetuosity
Stamping mine Age with magic,
Sing your song for the Ages to come.

Saraswathi, summer of my life!
Let us discuss intelligent ideas,
Let us dissect the poetics of Pandini,
&, if you deign to treat me,
Illuminate this speech,
Adorn my burning heart
With words of water, nectar, pomegranate -
To cleanse & clarify my lonely time-corner
In this poly-sided universe of things.

O, Saraswathi!
If, of India, I'll sing,
Give me the gifts of highest culture,
Of excellent temper, well-guarded,
Of winning manners & a handsome presence -
Indispensable assets of distinction.

Sing, Saraswathi, of the beaches of Gokarna,
& the rocky chain of crescents,
Where the Pterodactyls rose.

You saved my life, O Saraswathi! Twice!
Dragg'd me from a bus crash,
Steer'd me from a riptide,
I am your servant now, & so shall sing...

Saraswathi! Blessed anthropomorphic
Vision of incorporeal bliss,
A coming together of vague poetic forces,
In one iconic majesty,
I see thee, Goddess,
Dost thou see me?

Sing, Saraswathi, of the streets of Patiala,
Where the Jackson Pollock turbans
Of the Sikhs enliven days.

In painting we see the world others see,
In plays we meet our own experience,
In music we sense the universal soul,
In poetry our innermost thoughts express'd,
Secrets no longer, by everybody heard.

O, Saraswathi!
Let me handle the divine leaves
Of your fabulous Fifth Veda,
Beyond all mortal realms in scope & slokas,
Transcending all Earth's energies in style -
All-inclusively;
Sciences, philosophy, religious speculations!

O, Saraswathi! Precious Saraswathi!
What is Mahabharata?
Literature? Painting? Sculpture? Music?
Didactic molder of Mankind's character?
O! L et this epic perfect my searing soul!

O Saraswathi! Monarch of my Muses,
Take me to Vyasa,
Poet of the panthers,
Alive in Jaggernatha,
'Very well,' said Vyasa,
'I shall come here every day
To the same place, at the same time
With a hundred fresh sloka
Of my burgeoning Bharata song
Compos'd that very morning.'

O! Mahabharata! O! India!
Gigantic globe of thought enrob'd,
The Bharata Wars are the Universe,
Containing galaxies of narratives,
Forging consciousness in various spheres,
Finding ample sense in complex rhythms,
Where prospers humanity's myriads,
Puppets of psychological circumstance
Ethical speculations, great & small.

At a party for immortals,
Am I Bacchus of the Ganga?
Or Apollo of the Punjab?
Give me ink, & give me goat-skin,
Give me wine, find me Lucille,
To play us tender melodies
Upon your string'd sitar.

Sing, Saraswathi, the Song of the Lord,
The Gita of indestructible embodiment,
We shall not grieve for the dead,
We shall not mourn the dead with tears,
For they are still alive,
& there never was a time when they were not.

Give me, Saraswathi, as you gave to Vyasa,
The gift of sight, & in that seeing, beauty;
Fram'd by the imparting arts of poetry,
Let me mould my mimesi
Like rouge, clay cups containing India's chai.

Chai! Chai! Chai!
My train rumbles on,
Muttering, shuddering,
Thro' shutters I see...

Oh! renovated rotund of Kolkata!
Oh! pigeon-haunted rubbish tips!
Oh! rubber emporiums in the ruins of the Raj!

Look at the masses! Gaze on the multitudes!
Inflam'd with religion,
Mourning hagiographic reliquerie -
Ye Prophets of the West, your time has come,
See how scrivan godspell cast upon the Earth!

A question follows me everywhere,
'Are you married, sir?'
My reply always surprises,
'Yes... to Saraswathi!'

Upon the splendid esplanade of life,
Beside oceanic universe,
Poets walk, hand-in-hand,
With Muses, well-dress'd,
Paying off their soul-pledg'd Mit'a,
Passing multitudes of perfunctory pedestrians,
They sometimes draw deep, admiring glances
From those wishing deeply
To eavesdrop on conversations.
Because, *'what do Muses talk about*
When walking with their chosen,
Along splendid esplanades?'

Let all of us surrender to the Divine Will,
Fulfilling respective duties
To Karma-Yoga, to Sva-Dharma;
In the smoothest running of society
There is wrong action, there is inaction,
& there is the way of inscrutable action,
Devoid of motivating desires -
Renouncing attachments to fruits of action,
Ensures independence & contentment.

Calcutta! Cacophony!
Calliope's Conduit,
Clio's Accountant,
Altho' thou more a charnel house of madness,
Adore thee, I do, do I?

Two nations stand still -
India, Pakistan -
Embattl'd ball-by-ball;
TVs on chi-stalls,
Radios in bookshops,
Pregnant, panting pauses,
Girls & Boys,
Miseries & Joys...
When the last wicket falls, Kolkata erupts
In waves incredible celebrations.

Street level, pregnant with ghee,
Shady lanes of guava green,
Lepers point with gnarling hands
At useless legs,
Lemon sellers do a lively business,
The card school prioritizes higher antes,
&, for the busiest shoefixers,
Homeopathic minerals are working again.

Praise the thirteen siblings
Of Rabindranath Tagore;
Dwijendra, Satyendra, Himendra, Bivendra,
Saudamini, Jyotirindra, Sukamari, Dunyendra,
Saratkumari, Swanakumari, Barankumari
Somendra & Budhendra.

Praise the honour of Rabindranath Tagore,
Upon whose spirit all vidyas converge,
Whose village meant more than white glory,
Disavowing the punitive West,
Refusing an Emperor's knighthood.

Sing, Saraswathi, of white-wash'd Pondicherry,
& the mantric revelations
That you gave Sri Aurobindo,
Omniscient in syllabary!

O Beloved, My Beloved!
While I sing my song,
Plant for me a vineyard
With choicest branches of grape,
Build me a tower made of rachis,
& leave me a winepress near the garden
To boil my rustic wines.

& Saraswathi, be my lover too!
Let us make out passionately
In the long valley of the Durance,
Let me pleasure you
Like a Princess of Monaco,
Let me fuck you
Like a common Marseille whore.

I went to India,
& now possess a mind,
Under silken sari sooth'd,
Of the supreme artist intellect!

Sing, Saraswathi, of Siva's fiery lingam,
Atop Arunachala's mountain,
Oer Tiruvannamalai.

Yes, sing, Saraswathi,
Thro' the song which I am singing,
& the signs that we are bringing
To the gather'd hearers, here;
There is a light in the music,
There is life forever after,
In a song that's sung sincere.

ODES

ON

a

TOUR

of the

SICILIAN
ISLAND

of

MARETTIMO

Il mio giro di un'isola bella

One

Sicilia sublime
Cuore di oceano antico
Cucina di cultura

Animato Trapani
Smeraldo del Mediterraneo
Delizia di pescatori

L'onde riflettono il sole
Marettimo splendida estensione
La gente si avvicina al porto

Odore di pane cotto al forno
Caldi panini riempiono la mia borsa
Pizza per prima colazione

Galleria d'alberi
Gli uccelli cantano dolcezza
Pietroso paesaggio sale ripido

Gioco di rocce irregolare
Punta Bassano
Crocifisso del pescatore morto

Two

Passi di esse levarsi
Serpente zigzaga attraverso il paesaggio
Pini affollano la Carcaredda

Discendo alla spiaggia
Salto masso dopo masso
Lungo la baia forma d'arco

Roccia di marmo e rosa
Geologia dilettante
Acquaforte di tempo profondo

Scalo la Spalmatore
Sopra, un altro pianeta,
Oh! Quando il nostro mondo era giovane?

Suono spacca il silenzio
Aviogetto Italiano
Curva attraversa le scene

Pace poiche la mia anima,
Questo momento purifica,
Canta per la Sicilia

Three

Discendendo con il giorno
Da questa cresta d'edera
Crreo valanghe minuscole

Orrizonte rosa
Mare inghiotte il sole rosso
Stella di sera che si alza

Pericolosa passaeggiata
I Gabbiani molestano
Una barca da pesca sul mare

Vecchio Castello Spagnolo
Sella la schiena d'una tartaruga
Gemiti fanno eco dalla sua prigione

Stelle cominciano il loro regno
Capre fuggono al mio passaggio
Scorto la barca al paese

Nel bar della piazza animato
Leggo ad alta voce la mia poesia
Il mio giro di un'isola bella

TO

an

ENGLISHMAN

With

LIBERTY

EAST LOTHIAN

O soul-enchanting poesy,
Thou'st long been all the world with me
John Clare

*

Sir, did you please your skin 'neath Nunraw's sylvan falls,
Or ease your boat within old Dunbar's harbor walls,
& have you ever gazed on Whittinghame's strange yew
As morning's chorus lazed, drunk on a haar's fresh dew?

Sir, did you stroll the swerve serving Port Seton's sands,
Invested with the verve East Lothian demands,
Like pullin' young fungi from Saltoun's lofty wood,
Or gladly ambling by the Younger's handsome flood?

Sir, did you ever take the views from Deuchrie Dod,
& in that moment make a pact with Man & God,
To wander to & fro, record all felt & seen & felt,
Until thy senses flow from things that once have been.

To an Englishman with Liberty
Dost thou ken thy's a bard?
'I do, sir, in my dreams!'
You do? By land & sea
Ascend art's boulevard,
Upbending via beams
Thro' Heavens thickly starr'd!

CELTICA

*

Sir, did you ever take these bright isles in a tour,
The pride of Scotland slake on Hampden's awesome roar;
& did you ever stun the herds of Wicklow deer,
Or strike a mountain run on Snowdon sloping sheer?

Sir, have you spent a night with haggis Burns & song,
Or watch'd a ravensflight from battle cairns at Kong,
& have you seen the sun oer Glencoe's savagery,
Or seen Portmeirion In total privacy?

Sir, did you break your fast upon old Boney's nose,
Then gaze upon Belfast with all those terraced rows,
& have you ever stood atop the Isle of Man,
When weather fine & good, spreads Britain like a fan?

To an Englishman with Liberty
Ye love thy Celtic fringe?
'I do so, & am proud!'
You are? Then set life free,
Go let your soul impinge
Into thy native crowd,
Streaking a silver tinge.

ENGLAND

The country is looking much more beautiful
Edith Holden

*

Sir, have you ever seen Cumbria clad in snow,
Or Brighton's beaches been in summer's easy glow,
& have you ever heard the Cambridge matin bells,
Or felt your senses stirr'd when England's anthem swells?

Sir, did you drink the ale brew'd for the northern mills,
Or watch seafarers sail from Whitby's salty sills,
& did you ever feed your thirst in Cornish Springs,
Or take the time to read thro' histories of kings?

Sir, have you ever pass'd an afternoon at Lords,
Or watch'd a happy cast a-tread Adelphi's boards,
& have you ever cheer'd the horses round Aintree,
Or as a bargeman steer'd the waters of the Lea?

To an Englishman with liberty,
What of these coy demands?
'These things, sir, I have known!'
You have? Then let us fly
Beyond these fabled lands
The English call their own,
Set sail for Calais sands.

EUROPA

The tide is full, the moon lies fair
Matthew Arnold

*

Sir, did you ever ride the high-speed Gallic trains,
Or climb a mountainside kept by Croatian swains,
& did you ever try the tramways of Zurich,
Or skiing full hilt fly upon an Alpine peak?

Sir, did you ever tour the fields of Waterloo,
Or Rooney urge to score amidst a foreign crew,
& did you lap the flow of Castalian Spring,
Or seek a fireside glow from Finland's wintry sting?

Sir, did you ever dance with maidens of Seville,
Or breathe the elegance of the Avantine Hill,
& did you surf the scree barefoot upon the Basque,
Or taste the brevity of the Venetian masque?

To an Englishman with Liberty
Italy has it all,
'It does, sir, & does well!'
Bene! No finer place,
To forge a poet's soul,
'Tis here the Muses dwell,
& welcome one & all.

ITALIA

Paradise of Exiles
PB Shelley

*

Sir, did your pallet taste sepia's sable sheen,
Or spread green pesto paste on bread like margarine,
Did you Collodi climb to read Pinnochio,
Or see day set sublime oer Pontevecchio?

Sir, did you pace the maze thro' old Venetian lanes,
Or gulp down as you gaze on Pompeii's strange remains,
& did you ever take the waters of Trieste,
Or swim Averno's lake without a moment's rest?

Sir, did you cheer the riffs as Ligabue rocks,
Walk Cinque Terran cliffs, or bought Le Scale box,
& did you deck the sails by Ponza's pirate isle,
Or study Tuscan tayles in Dante's sweet new style?

To an Englishman with Liberty
Art thou adventurous
'I am sir, life is good!'
It is? then reach this sea
The gods named glorious,
Let freedom clasp thy hood,
& cross the Bosporus.

GLOBAL

In view and opposite two cities stood
Christopher Marlowe

*

Sir, did you feel the heat of searing Rajhastan,
Or clad kimono greet fair geishas of Japan,
& did you ever wear th'Atlantic's mistral miles,
Or dreams of Zion share about Samoan isles?

Sir, did you ever ride the Vladivostok rail,
Or watch the proud roos hide from harsh Van Diemen hail,
& did you ever climb the Islandwhanan rock,
Or hear the lilting chime of Ganzhou's epic clock?

Sir, did you note the chill of the Saharan night,
Or felt your senses thrill with Rio neath your flight,
& did you ever smell the waifs of Singapore,
Or share a living hell when nations go to war?

To an Englishman with Liberty
With spirit cavalier,
For you the world grows dull?
'It does!' Then come with me,
A fresher course to steer,
Launch from Canaveral,
To chase the stratosphere.

SOLARIS

Their lives for the cause
Astronauts Memorial

*

Sir, did you foot the floor of dusty lunar seas,
Or spread your mind & soar upon the solar breeze,
& did you ever sail betwixt the Saturn rings,
Or catch a comet's tail & tie it to your wings?

Sir, did you abseil down craters of Mercury,
Or wander rusting towns of Martian history,
& did you pierce the clouds 'twixt Ceres & Trojan,
Or hide beneath the clouds of rains Venusian?

Sir, did you feel winds form on Neptune's azure reed,
Or watch the great red storm from twinkling Ganymede,
& did you once observe the green Urasian glow,
Then with Colombus verve pass fringes of Pluto?

To an Englishman with Liberty
Have you these pleasures sought?
'I have sir, & have felt!'
God bless astronomy!
Relax, come let us float,
Beyond the Kuiper belt,
Upon our blazing boat.

SEDNA

*

Sir, have you ever gone beyond the icy Quaoar,
Or paused at Ixion, core of an ancyent star,
& did you scan the skies, lovely, from Varuna,
Or set your naked eyes on sanguineous Sedna?

Sir, come with us & spin upon this scarlet sphere,
Thro' head of tiny pin watch this vast sun appear,
Here ye shall find no guide, nor shall ye hear a sound,
From Sedna's swirling side a rocky moon slips round.

Sir, watch the goddess sit, voluptuous & fair,
Beloved Enuit, with starfish-dappl'd hair,
Whom by her husband cruel purg'd of all vanities,
Now sits she as the jewel of the infinities...

To an Englishman with Liberty
What brings ye to this place?
'She called me from her stone!'
She did? Then cross this sea
She calls the stretch of space,
Continue, sir, alone
A vapor without trace.

GALAXIA

Rapturous flowers of the soul
Sri Aurobindo

*

Sir, feel each sphere that forms as if life's hallow'd birth,
Faint, incandescent storms enough to swallow Earth,
& let us delve along distances none conceive,
Some durable among extremes none dare believe.

So many rocks like ours, some more Peg Fifty-One,
Whom in a hundred hours will hurtle around her sun,
Stars flicker firefly by supernovae gongs,
While choirs of nebulae court angels with sad songs;

Sir, witness Icarus, a single stable star,
Whose supergiant dress our furthest light by far,
Here nature helter-skelts! Here cosmos skirls askew!
Here conscious motion melts in pools of pearly blue!

To an Englishman with Liberty
Freed feel thee from this cage?
'I do, Sir, like a bird!'
You are? Then let us flee,
Forever on this page,
Untether'd from the herd,
A jester on the stage.

ON

the

JUNKIE
FUCKS

of

LEITH

He tried to tear the horror from himself,
Searching in the sockets of his eyes with needles
Till they burst blood
The Phoenician Woman

Strophe

There's a Junkie Fuck
Everywhere you look
: in Leith

Great Junkie Street
Five-minutes-to-midnight
Zombie-crowded cash-machines

Kids like, *'Where's-my-crack-pipe?'* boy
Grinnin' into school
Thinkin' he was cool

'I'm never injecting,' he blusters upsetly
Blazin' about his Best Friend's funeral:
At the Wake… to ease his grief… shoots up first time!

His crack-whore *'Wudya,'* works Leith Links's edges
A posh-painted Picture pick'd up by drunk dockers
While her daughter chews straws at McDonalds

Her looks are fading, she turns to friends
Getting them hooked so maybe they'll pay
For these needles fresh 'besties' dare share

There's a Smackie Kunt
Always on the hunt
: in Leith

Antistrophe

There's a Junkie Worm
Every corner turn'd
: in Leith

The Skag is a slippery, shrieking Beast
Cunning as Fox, strong as Lion
Foul as farting Pig

Don't listen to what they say, but how they say it,
Bullshit Defence Mechanism takes control
Insidious serpent contorting thought

How the hell can ya call it glamorous?
When glamping means begging up the North Bridge
Contemplating suicide in torn, soggy shoes

Viledom's finest scourge Leith Walk
Piping, *'We are young… We can handle it…'*
'…We could drop it just like that.'

But when they join the clucking Cold Turkeys
& Methadone Monkeys in gibbering clinics
It's more *{ { p e a c e f u l } }* just to try it one last time

There's a Bag-Head Prick
Itching itself sick
: in Leith

Epode

There's a Junkie Fool
Shuffling past yer school
: in Leith

I was twenty-one once,
Busking down Bournemouth
Boozing wi' beggars

I'd follow'd 'em into a nappy-dirty yard
Watching 'em cook up their hard-earned stuff
& said, *'I'll have a go,'* in all innocence

'You don't wanna try,' said Feathers,
'Do I not?… alright…' three days later
I found him overdosing in his tent

Never babysit a Smack-Head!
If you show signs of weakness they will take
& take & take & lie & take & steal & take & scrounge
& take & lie & steal & take & scrounge & take &…

…when you've stopp'd giving they'll turn round & hiss,
'I thought you were my friend?'

There's a Junkie Shmuck
Lonely, Soul-less, Stuck
: in Leith

FREE VERSE

THE LOST POEM

I wrote a poem once,

At Stockport, not far from the gates of Europa

My friend was driving there one sunny day

Smoking reefers & talking about life's changes

We ended up in a funky metal scrapyard

One of those places you never thought existed

Like when you were younger & joked

About where all the lost odd socks went

But this place was the real deal,

Full of Volkswagen carcasses,

Camper vans & Beetle hulks

A couple of greasy mechanics, chilling with the sun

While Nicky looked at a ninety-nicker bumper

I was suddenly inspired to write a few desolate lines

About decaying Earth

& the dwindling fuel reserves

& finished it off with an arty kind of twist

About discovering an old photograph of myself

Holding a young lady, she was wearing beads

Sat upon the beach of, perhaps, San Remo...

...All that never really happen'd,

But all poems need an end!

So I stashed it away,

A single sheet of paper folded several times

Constantly forgetting to type the blighter up

Until it turned up in a book I was reading

Livy's remarkable *Early History of Rome*

I'd packed it on my mission round the Baltic

Where, trawling about the soft streets of Stockholm

Wondering what the hell the plastic cows were for

Every time I picked it up the sheet fell out the pages

Constantly reminding me that I should make it safe

It'd only take a second, but I never took the time...

I found myself having one of those moments

Sun setting sublimely as I made my evening meal

On the forecastle of the hotel boat I was staying on

The splish-splosh of waves & a gust of sea breeze

Blew out the sheet as I turned a page

To float on the air like a falling feather

Time was standing still, the paper started **F**

                                                 A

Slips thro' the narrowest of cracks between **L** boards

To be found one day in the distant future   **L**

 By someone breaking up the hold for scrap   **I**

                                                    N

                                                    G

From Stockport to Stockholm flew my fine words

& now I've gone & bloody lost 'em!

I was well gutted at first,

Like the time my girlfriend ran off with a German

But, as I ponder'd home to my cabin empty-handed,

Past painted memorials of the age of sail

I had a remarkable epiphany

        At last my poem had a proper end!

THE LAST POEM

I wrote a poem once,

Among foliage flocking to reptile rocks,

Listening to the Goat bell tinnitus,

Penetrate birdsong silence.

At PRIVADO bravado fences,

I make my primitive bouquets,

Feed donkeys handfuls of dandelions.

Laid back & lazy,

Several miles from the Real Cartuja

& the Moors of the Musa valley,

A little extra to the Grave of Graves -

'Ozymandias, King of Kings!'

Shelley's ever living sonnet

Mi accompagna sul sentiero

Fill'd up with a leadbelly breadbelly,

Esporles to Banyalbalfur,

When sun of Spring settles on such scenes

Unveils a very heaven!

Twisted olive trees;

Electric shocks of jazz-green hair,

Like Gustave Dore's depiction

Of Dante's fallen souls,

March like Ents thro' the bidden groves.

Descending to Banyanbalfur,

Ski-slope steep,

Swathes of sea & verdancy,

Skipping among beauty

I muse on the new mantras of my life.

Has it really been a quarter century

Since first I felt my miracle Muse

Blissfully free by the palaces of Pisa?

There is energy in my stride,

As if I'd heard the Yankee band,

Cover'd with French flowers,

Marching down the Rue de Rivoli,

Escorted by a sweeping crowd,

Under the great iron fence of the Tuileries.

I reach the beacon of my long endeavor;

Where, settling on a terrace with a beer,

I'll a quarter century's compositions -

At last! At last! At last! At last! At last!

My poems had their proper, precious end!

NOTES TO THE POEMS

THE CANZONE

Love At First Sight (2004/2012): Six of the stanzas were compos'd during one of my 'mojo' periods when the ladies were into me & I into them (I was 27). At the end of these romantic sessions, I settl'd into a committed relationship with a farmer's daughter from Dumfries, Glenda Rome, moving into her flat on Scotland Street in Edinburgh. A decade later, after my relationship with Glenda had broken down, & upon meeting Miss Elinor Dickie in Edinburgh, two more stanzas were added to the poem.

What Bleeds For Five Days (& Does Not Die?) (2006): Compos'd in Marettimo, December, in response to one of the more vicious menstrual explosions which erupted from my first long-term partner, Glenda. Believe you me, she wasn't very happy when I read it out to her not long after it's composition was completed.

To the 250,000 victims... (2004): Compos'd in the immediate aftermath of the Boxing Day tsunami that struck the Indian Ocean.

Paisley (2006): Compos'd cathartically not long after the incident describ'd. I have return'd to Paisley in 2022, to visit a young lady, which presented me with better memories of Scotland's largest town.

THE BALLADS

The Ballad of Rabbie Burns (2009): An edited version of a ballad cycle compos'd to commemorate the 'Homecoming' celebration held in Scotland in honour of the 250th anniversary of the birth of Scotia's holy bard,

Matty Grooves (2017): A transcreation of a traditional English folk song, moving the setting from the Medieval era to the contemporary Edinburgh club scene.

Over the Top (2021/22): Taken from the ballad cycle, *'Black Watch Brodick.'* Compos'd at Fell View, Arran, in the house next door to the Brodick War memorial, this section is set on the morning of the Battle of Loos, September 25th, 1915.

The Battle of Chester (2004/2005): Originally composed upon visiting the 4000 year-old cairns & monuments of Cong, during a tour of the West of Ireland with Glenda. A year later, I mov'd the setting of the poem to the Anglo-Saxon conquest of England.

The Ballad of Pendle Hill (2010): A heavily edited down version of a ballad cycle compos'd in tribute to my home town of Burnley's principle lore & legend, the witch trials of 1612.

The Golgog of Glen Rosa (2022): Compos'd quite spontaneously on Arran during a period of True Crime fandom.

THE SONNETS

Modern Life (1998): Compos'd as part of the Sable Rose grand sequence of sonnets, in order to mark the age into which I had launch'd my poetical spirit.

This Is My Country (2003): Compos'd in the New Town of Edinburgh after visiting Glenda Rome, a lady I had just started seeing. It was originally an opening invocation to the Bohemia sequence I penn'd on a multi-legg'd journey from Edinburgh to London, in the Autumn of 2003, edited down to sonnet form at a later date.

Training in the Art of Fare Evasion (2001): A list sonnet into which has been recorded, rather like an Ashokan edict, the chief dogmatic tenets of the Way of the Fader – i.e. the Fare Evader. In the year 2001 I was at the peak of my powers in this noble art form, being able to ride the rails of Britain & Continental Europe at will, & for free.

Westenders (2001): A memorial to a fine evening with a lovely young lady. In 2001 I was living in Tunbridge Wells, working on the World War Two sections of my epic poem, Axis & Allies, which would not be completed until 2020.

Rosie's School Run (2018): Inspir'd by witnessing the manic energies surrounding the morning school run to Yester Primary School in East Lothian, both thro' Emily's eyes & that of Kenny Curran.

Recollections - First Kiss (2004): Compos'd as part of a sequence of sonnets dedicated to my earliest girlfriends. The actual name of the girl is long lost to me, but the memory of our time together is still vivid.

Mi Dad (2014): Compos'd on my return to Burnley & subsequent domiciling in his house on Athletic Street for a wee while. What a guy!

Skye (2003): Compos'd upon from my first trip to Skye, which had been instigated by Glenda. Not long after we had set off back to Edinburgh from Portree, we reach'd the road thro' the Cuillin Hills where the poem was created.

A Day in the Life of Love (2016): Compos'd Baro Farm Cottages, East Lothian, for Emily, not long after we had set up home there.

Edinburgh Zoo (2010): From the Ediniad grand sequanza of poems, & one I just really enjoy!

Vagabondo (2004): My first attempt at creating something like a poem in the Italian language, made more interesting by my use of the 11th century Sicilian version of the sonnet.

Hell's Gates (2006): Part of a longer, but incomplete sequence, compos'd in response to the death of my darling Grandmother, Joan Sumner, in the February of 2006. The idea was to reach via Dante's Heaven.

Below Scopello (2006): Another Sicilian version of the sonnet form, compos'd in Sicily itself. After Palermo, Scopello was the first place Glenda & I stay'd in upon our Mediterranean winter.

Castalian Spring (2011): Compos'd at Delphi after filling a water bottle with the legendary poetry-fueling waters of the Castalian Spring. Not far away uprose the wooded slopes of Mount Parnassus, the main beacon of my pilgrimage to Greece.

The Incredible India Code (2002): Compos'd from experience throughout my first tour in India, January-April, 2002.

The Ear Cleaner (2002): The events describ'd occur'd in my first ever week on my first ever trip to the sub-continent. The composition of the poem soon follow'd.

Poverty & Wealth (2010): One of my favorite sonnets, compos'd upon my 4th tour in India, winter 2010-11.

Creation (2008): Compos'd after witnessing the describ'd scene on the streets of Canacona, Goa. During the later assembling of the *Indiad* grand sonnet sequanza, the sonnet's setting was mov'd to Mumbai.

THE EPYLLIA

The Grand Tour (1998): Compos'd in Portsmouth, a year after the events describ'd, in a more polish'd form of Ottava Rima

Squatting London (2003): Part of my 'Bohemia' sequence of Free Verse poems compos'd upon a tour of Britain. The sonnet, *'This is my Country'* was originally part of the same sequence.

The Honeymoon (2016): An extract of a longer poem compos'd in the Autumn & Winter of 2016, during which time Emily & I visited Europe & America. On the European leg we both visited Paris for the first time, having both waited to find true love before we could honestly visit the most romantic city in the world.

THE CANTATA

Song of the Morning (2023): Compos'd in the run up to the publication of this book. Inspir'd by a number of entries in a series of Francis Gay's *'Friendship Books,'* which I was selling in my 'Nine Bees' bookshop, on the Isle of Arran.

Saraswathi Song (2011/13/23): Initially compos'd in Calcutta, 2011, as study notes on paper in absence of a laptop. Two years later a number of stanzas were compos'd on a tour of Britain, which was blended with the 2011 work & added with new material in the run up to the publication of this book.

THE ODES

On a tour of... Marettimo (2006-07): Compos'd upon the Sicilian island of Marettimo, while wintering there with Glenda. This is an edited down version of a longer haiku sequence originally compos'd in English, then translated into Italian.

To an Englishman with Liberty (2004/2017):
Chiefly compos'd in London in early 2004 on the
announcement of the discovery of what was
consider'd to be, at that time, the tenth planet of
the solar system. Both Sedna, as the 'planet' was
call'd, & Pluto, were later relegated to mere
planetoid status. This first & last stanzas were
added at Carfrae, near Garvald, in East Lothian.

On the Junkie Fucks of Leith (2014): Compos'd
after a rather unpleasant flat share with a heroin
user at Pilrig Park apartments, Edinburgh.

FREE VERSE

The Lost Poem (2004): Compos'd in Stockholm &
Tallinn during the immediate aftermath of the
original poem describ'd in the text.

The Last Poem (2023): Compos'd on the 18th April,
2023, on a walk from Esporles to Banyanbalfur.